PRAISE FOR
HOW WE LOVE

'An act of exquisite beauty, generosity and vulnerability from a woman who can also throw a fridge into the back of a car, all by herself. Big-hearted, fierce, tender, and so full of hope, just when we need it.'

Clare Bowditch, author of *My Own Kind of Girl*

'Gorgeous, immersive and deeply reassuring, *How We Love* reminded me once again how valuable and precious it is to find the words for the ways we love, and to share them.'

Sofie Laguna, author of *Infinite Splendours*

'Sensitive, soulful and utterly captivating. *How We Love* manages to be both beautiful and brutal, at the same time. Clem gives us words for the loves we've never been able to speak about before.'

Jamila Rizvi, author and editor of *The Motherhood*

'Everything in *How We Love* pierced me as I read—the humour, the honesty, the blistering detail. I laughed, and my heart ached . . . *How We Love* balances the specific and the universal so beautifully. It illuminates Clementine's experience, and sheds a light on us all.'

Alice Robinson, author of *The Glad Shout*

'A wise, tender and generous book about the agonies and ecstasies of being a human who dares to love. At once intimate and universal, *How We Love* is an ode to opening our hearts, again and again—despite knowing that pain awaits. Ford reminds us that, even when they hurt, our feelings are the very meat of life.'

Yves Rees, author of *All About Yves: Notes from a Transition*

'How can stories from someone else's life make you feel so seen, so known, so bloody tender towards your younger self? That's the power of great memoir and *How We Love* is glorious. Sparkling prose, heart-in-mouth honesty and Clementine's trademark wit, warmth and sincerity. I laughed, I cried, I cringed, I forgave myself a hundred times. You'll fall in love with Clementine just a little bit more.'

Karen Pickering, writer and feminist communicator

PRAISE FOR
FIGHT LIKE A GIRL

'Brilliant . . . it makes me want to chain myself to a barricade.'

Tracey Spicer, *Sun-Herald*

'Clementine Ford was put on this earth to give courage to the young girl inside all of us. This is an exciting, essential book from Australia's most fearless feminist writer.'

Laurie Penny, author of *Unspeakable Things*

'I'm going to come right out and say it: Clementine Ford's *Fight Like A Girl* should be required reading for all young women in Australia . . . Reading *Fight Like A Girl* reignited my feminist fire, my feelings of frustration . . . Yes, *Fight Like A Girl* will make you angry. It will make you feel uncomfortable. But, ultimately, it will inspire you to create change.'

Marie Claire

'Clementine is furious and scathing when she needs to be, yet compassionate and encouraging every moment she can be. This book is both a confirmation of sisterhood and a call to arms.'

Bri Lee, author of *Eggshell Skull* and *Who Gets to Be Smart?*

'*Fight Like A Girl* should be required reading for every young man and woman, a brave manifesto for gender equality, harm minimisation and self-care.'

Clare Wright, *The Australian*

'Australian feminist Clementine Ford is never one to shy away from combat or controversy, and her first book, *Fight Like A Girl*, is a fierce and personal call to arms in the campaign for women's rights . . . *Fight Like A Girl* is an important book for Australians young and old, and for burgeoning activists.'

Stephanie Van Schilt, *The Australian*

'A potent mix of memoir and manifesto, equal parts fierce and friendly; an intimate, witty self-portrait and a rousing call to arms for women everywhere to know their rage, own it, wear it and channel it into fighting for change.'

Sydney Morning Herald, The Age **and** *Canberra Times*

'*Fight Like A Girl* is fuelled by Ford's clear-eyed defiance and refusal to compromise, and by her powerful combination of personal testimony and political polemic. In the vein of Caitlin Moran's *How to be a Woman* or Roxane Gay's *Bad Feminist*.'

Books + Publishing

'Brutally honest and unapologetic . . . Ford tackles society's double standards and contradictions, tackling these head-on like a fearless heroine . . . *Fight Like A Girl* is a feisty call to arms for modern women . . . Keep on fighting the good fight, Clem, so that one day we may all enter the ring with you.'

AU Review

'Clementine Ford was one of my very first formative feminist influences, initiating me into the world of feminism. She is someone whose tenacity and fearlessness I admire greatly, and she helped me along the path to becoming the humourless, bitter, lesbian feminist I am today.'

Rebecca Shaw, writer, SBS and
WomanAgainstFeminism@NoToFeminism

'A beautiful, bittersweet journey to self-acceptance. A companion to all those still seeking to forge a sense of self. Clementine Ford has always been a bastion of shamelessness in a world that would rather see her defeated, and her book is a testament to the commitment she has to living fearlessly. I am comforted daily by her presence in the lives of young Australians, and I'm beyond thrilled that we now have her unique brilliance committed to these pages.'

Caitlin Stasey, actor and creator of Herself.com

'As a feminist writer, Clementine has placed great importance on establishing and maintaining a strong connection with the women's services sector, and to those who do the work supporting women experiencing male violence. The women's services sector places great value on Clementine's writing, and that the relationship is mutually beneficial really speaks to Clementine's values. The past few years have been a watershed for the elimination of violence against women in Australia, and Clementine's voice has not only been instrumental, but has taken up a mainstream space that has aligned with and reinforced the efforts of the women's services sector. We love her for that.'

Ada Conroy, family violence worker

'It's a call to action but, more importantly, it's a call to reason. A must-read for all women.'

Fashion Journal

Clementine Ford is a writer and broadcaster living on Wurundjeri country in Naarm/Melbourne. *How We Love* is her third book.

CLEMENTINE FORD

HOW WE LOVE

NOTES ON A LIFE

ALLEN&UNWIN
SYDNEY·MELBOURNE·AUCKLAND·LONDON

First published in 2021

Allen & Unwin
83 Alexander Street
Crows Nest NSW 2065
Australia
Phone: (61 2) 8425 0100
Email: info@allenandunwin.com
Web: www.allenandunwin.com

A catalogue record for this
book is available from the
National Library of Australia

ISBN 978 1 76087 718 7

Set in 12/19 pt Warnock Pro Light by Bookhouse, Sydney
Printed in Australia by McPherson's Printing Group

10 9 8 7 6 5 4 3

The paper in this book is FSC® certified.
FSC® promotes environmentally responsible,
socially beneficial and economically viable
management of the world's forests.

FOR ALICE

CONTENTS

INTRODUCTION

I was twenty-one when I fell in love for the first time.

I'm talking real, proper love. The kind of love that feels messy and painful, but also illuminating and world-changing. She was in Adelaide for the weekend, and we met at a dinner party held by a former housemate of mine. When I arrived, she was standing in the courtyard outside the kitchen, smoking a cigarette. We all smoked cigarettes back then, rolling them deftly over pub tables and share house couches while talking animatedly about feminism, student politics and who had been evicted from *Big Brother* that week. I immediately began a loud conversation with the host, who was pulling something out of the oven, or perhaps making a salad or pouring a drink.

'Where's this friend of yours that you want me to meet, then?' I asked, reaching for a glass of wine or a piece of cheese or maybe a pouch of tobacco.

The friend poked her head through the door, the tip of the cigarette burning red against the dark hedge behind her, and introduced herself.

Later, I would tell people that I had known something was going to happen that night. I'd known it in the way we always seem to after the event, because nothing guides us more in love than our belief in it. We might forget the details, but never the way they made us feel. In one of the long letters we wrote to each other, she told me she heard my voice before she saw my face. I read her letters and reread them, holding them gently but firmly for fear that a sudden breeze might sweep them away.

But before this, on the night of the happening, I joined her outside. We smoked cigarettes and chatted, and I tried to ignore the flutter of wings coming to life in my tummy. Less than three hours later, we were in bed together.

Despite having kissed women, I had yet to sleep with one. I'd imagined the experience countless times, of course, but I'd expected to be more terrified by the mechanics of it. In the moment, though, nothing could have been easier. Afterwards, we curled into each other and lay that way throughout the night. The next morning, our parting was heavy with melancholy. She was returning to Melbourne that afternoon, and it would be a while before I'd see her again.

In the interim, we did what people separated by distance have always done to keep the home fires burning: we wrote letters and slipped them into envelopes along with trinkets and treats we thought the other person would like. While we waited for the letters to arrive, we sent emails and spoke for hours on the phone, pulling blankets and cordless landlines into our backyards at midday and talking until the sun had moved almost completely across the sky and the chill of evening had set in. Eventually, we began travelling by bus to see each other. Back then, you could get a return ticket to Melbourne for $39 (or was it $59?), and the nine-hour journey across flat, brown land seemed infinitely worth it. I read a lot of Jodi Picoult books during those transits—thick tomes with comfortably predictable storylines that were just compelling enough to make the time go faster.

How many cups of tea did we share, sitting on porches, talking about books and music and what we wanted to be when we grew up, despite playing at being grown-ups already? It must have been over one of those brews that she told me something I've always remembered: falling in love is really about discovering yourself and who you are.

I'd thought myself in love before, with various boys. Quiet boys; gregarious boys; boys caught between the soft roundness of youth and the rough edges of manhood; boys who didn't know I existed and seemed likely to remain ignorant to me forever; boys who did know me but would have preferred not to; boys who probably liked me back but were too scared of what their friends would think to do anything about it; boys who were gay and wrestling with unrequited love of their own. So many boys, whose shadows I followed through the grim valleys and dramatic peaks of adolescence, wanting more than anything for them to turn towards me and bathe me in their light.

I loved in the way that teenagers so often do—uncritically, desperately and with the singular desire to be loved in return. I wanted to be seen and understood as a person in the world, someone who existed beyond the sphere of her family and all the ways you can be simultaneously known and not known within that dynamic.

This desire plagued the interactions I'd had with my first boyfriend, who I dated for a few months during my second year at university. He was funny and bouncy, but most importantly he was almost as inexperienced as I was when it came to the merging of two lives into one, and in this sense he felt safe. We kissed for the first time in a half-built house on my street. We went there one night in a group, ten or so of us drunkenly stumbling from my porch to traipse around the death trap like childish buffoons. He grabbed my hand as I fell up the concrete stairs that sat in the middle of the unfinished structure, and when he kept holding it even after I'd righted myself I let myself believe, perhaps for the first time, that this was a thing I was allowed to want.

When I told him I loved him a few months later, he replied, 'Thank you.' He said the same thing whenever I tried to coax a similar declaration from him, and each time I grew more humiliated. When he broke up with me, explaining that his inability to reciprocate my feelings was nothing to do with me but, rather, evidence of some *dark turmoil* within him, I wept on the phone to my mother.

'Mummy, I *love* him!' I wailed, wounded yet secretly enraptured by the performance of my own heartbreak.

'Don't be silly!' she laughed, which of course made me feel even sillier.

When the woman and I fell out of love a few years after this, it wasn't with the same torment of the soul I'd felt at nineteen. There were no explosive fights or fits of rage. Our love didn't turn toxic or bitter, so that the qualities we had previously found charming about each other now seemed obnoxious and irritating. We'd had a moment, perfect and profound in its own way, but temporary, and we both knew it. The sun rose and moved languidly across the sky, a day filled with promise stretching out before us. But the shadows grew longer, as they always do, and at some point we turned away from each other in the dark, and woke to find each other gone.

And yet, some essence of the love remains, just as it has done for all the people and things and moments I have loved in my life whose time has come to an end. Because I didn't just fall in love with her that year. I fell in love with Melbourne, whose dinging tram bells heralded each arrival into the city—the city that would soon enough become my home too, and in which I would love and be loved many times over. I remember the sausage rolls we had one day at Sugardough on Lygon Street; I only ate them that once, but I can still recall the flaky, buttery pastry melting in my mouth. I remember Lucie Thorne, whose album formed the soundtrack of our love affair, and a pair of cheap beige shorts I wore one afternoon as we ran across the Fitzroy Gardens, and my legs felt strong and powerful and the two of us together untouchable. I think of the courage I'd had to summon to tell my parents about her, and the slight sliver of disappointment on realising they weren't overly concerned about my big revelation. I remember the fight we had after a party she took me to, only to disappear with a boy she worked with. I was wounded by it—but I was jealous too, because it reminded me of the stark difference between us, and how it seemed likely that people would always find her more beautiful than me. There were the diary entries I wrote when I moved to Japan for a year; long, pining entries about how much I missed her which grew fewer and farther between until they stopped altogether, life having decided to intervene and drag me back to the present.

It was a different time, as all times are.

I remember her fondly, but perhaps more than anything I remember the person I became while I was with her. To know love is to know more of yourself. This is what keeps us returning to all that it promises us. We desire to know ourselves more, and for that to happen we need to be *seen*.

I am a person who has loved deeply, strangely and with curiosity, a fact that may surprise some people. I am fascinated by love and the multiple ways it makes its home in our hearts. To continue to surrender ourselves to love, knowing as we do that it is a constantly changing, twisting beast that sometimes soothes us and at other times threatens to destroy us, is an act of great faith and bravery. When I was younger, I made the mistake of thinking love was a matter of being chosen; that romantic love was the only kind that had the capacity to profoundly change our lives, and that in this sense it was the only kind that mattered. Now that I have reached my middle years, I am able to see things more clearly. We love as children, as friends, as parents and, yes, sometimes as sexual beings, and none of it is more important than any of it, because all of it shows us who we are.

This is a book about love. It is not a book about *how* to love. It is not a book concerned with the scientific aspects of love. No research was conducted in the writing of this book, save for some very careful forensic examination of my own life. There is no data in this book, no useful statistics with which one may prove a point. Some of it will make you laugh. Some of it will make you cry. Unlike my previous work, I hope that rather than feeling angered by what this book reveals about the world we live in, you will instead be comforted by the fact that we still *live* in spite of it all.

If you have come to this book because you've read *Fight Like A Girl* and/or *Boys Will Be Boys*, you will see a different side to me. I hope, more than anything, that you won't be disappointed to learn of my emotional fallibilities as a human. That is, I hope it won't feel like a betrayal to discover that I too, have cried over people who didn't love me back, that I sometimes feel lonely and sad, and that beneath my seemingly hard exterior lies the same blood, bones and beating heart that exists in everyone.

This is a book about life, and all the ways we can be broken and pieced back together. It is a book about *my* life, which may in some places look an awful lot like yours.

I am almost certain all of it is true.

Clementine Ford
2021

1

THE STARSHIPS
ARE BURNING

When we were children, my siblings and I used to sleep with words under our pillows. It was something our mother taught us, slipping picture books and then early readers and finally chapter books beneath our heads before turning out the light.

'This way,' she'd tell us, 'the stories will find their way into your dreams.'

For years, I thought this was where everyone kept their books at night. I didn't realise it was a practice peculiar to our family, or that there were some people who didn't read books at all. We had grown up surrounded by books, hundreds of them spilling out of shelves and forming piles on the floor. My mother's tastes varied wildly; she read everything from the collected works of

Shakespeare to the crime novels of Ruth Rendell. She devoured books on politics and history, and was able to speak on these matters with an authority and confidence that belied her lack of a formal education.

Reading was never discouraged in our house, not even if it was done after lights out. If anything, we were often chided for reading what my mother thought were Bad Books. It pained her that I, a ten-year-old, wanted to read 'frivolous rubbish' like *The Baby-Sitters Club* and *Sweet Valley High*. She seemed to take it as a personal failing that any child of hers would dull their mind with stories about other girls their age, who navigated strained relationships at school and had crushes on sweet boys with floppy hair and shy smiles. Clearly, the only literary men worth pining after were those whom we could succeed in changing (Mr Darcy), those we could succeed in taming (Mr Rochester) and those we could succeed in haunting long after we had died and they'd decided to fully lean into their natural identity as a psychopath (Heathcliff).

After her death from cancer at the age of fifty-eight, my siblings and I took our turns rifling through her library, selecting the books we wanted to keep to read for ourselves, those we'd read and already loved, and those that we knew would just remind us of her. Some of the books were older than us, older even than her marriage to our father, which was as old as we'd ever really let ourselves think of her, women's lives so often being assumed to begin when they merge with a man's.

But as we pored through her collection in the wake of her death, we understood something we'd always skipped over before. These stories belonged to a different woman from the one we knew and loved. They belonged to a secret woman, the one who had signed her name *Luciana Gouveia* in blue ink in the top right-hand corner of the title page. These were the books she'd read when she was our age, younger even, dreaming of a world beyond her own and a life she might still get to live, even though it sometimes seemed to keep moving further and further out of reach.

We each have so many potential lives, and yet most of us only get to experience one or two of them. My mother was a million possible women all at once. I had only just begun to understand that in the months before she died, when the years of adolescent anger had fallen away and I could finally see a path to the place where we might meet as equals.

She was a woman filled with stories. Here is one of them.

❦

I was born in a tiny hospital in Miles, way out in the sprawling landscape of western Queensland. The sky burns red at sunset there even in the dead of winter, which is when my heavily pregnant mother sat down to play cards and continue the gruelling wait for labour to begin. I was a week overdue by now, my mother suspended in that strange space that exists between life and not-yet-life. She had resigned herself to another long stretch of nothing happening, and made herself a cup of tea in preparation.

Less than twelve hours later, as the dark liquid of night faded to the milky grey of dawn, I came tumbling into the world.

I know this story well. My mother told it every year on my birthday, as she did with the birth stories of all three of her children. I welcomed each rendition with the breathless anticipation of a child on Christmas morning, knowing exactly what to expect but still crinkling with excitement as though hearing it all for the first time.

The roots of this borrowed memory have been tended so carefully that I can picture it as if I were there. My parents sitting at the kitchen table in the cottage on my grandparents' farm, their card game still going strong at midnight. My mother's belly pressing against the wood, one hand gripping the mug that rests on top of the swell. Suddenly, the thin membrane that separates me from the world breaks and water bursts forth. Pain grips my mother in a vice. Oh, that pain! Despite having done this twice before, she's forgotten exactly what the pain of childbirth feels like.

Don't we all?

'Nature finds a way to make us do it again,' she told me years later.

When the contractions settle into a steady, torturous rhythm, they drive to the local hospital. The doctor arrives, and he tells my father to go home.

'It'll be hours yet!' he says confidently. 'You should go and get some rest!'

It's a short drive from Miles Hospital to the farm. My father has just climbed into bed when the phone rings to let him know it's all over. Luciana has given birth to a girl, and he had better come back.

'They're both fine,' the doctor says. 'It's all very normal.'

'You were born with jaundice,' my mother always said at this point. 'You came out bright yellow!'

The jaundice itself was fairly common, but the treatment required me to lie in an incubator for the first twenty-four hours of my life. The nurse had bandaged my eyes to protect them from the bright lights that were beaming down on me, but my mother was anxious that the makeshift blindfold would somehow slip off.

'I sat with you that whole time,' she would recall. 'I didn't trust the nurse to notice if something went wrong, and I was terrified your tiny little eyes would be exposed to the light.'

Perhaps this explains the irrational fear I've always had of losing my eyesight? It's funny. Until I wrote this story down, it never even occurred to me that the two could be connected. Trauma lies dormant for years before choosing to reveal itself in strange and unexpected places.

But, then, childbirth has always been a dangerous business. When my older brother was born, my mother suffered a massive haemorrhage and almost died in a pool of her own blood. This was part of his story, and every year I'd gasp at the telling, titillated by the excitement of it all. *She almost died!* I'd think to myself. *Like a character in a book! What a twist!*

Later, after the birth of my own son, when my own haemorrhage found me lying in a pool of my own blood, I thought about what that third and final journey into the mystery must have felt like for her. Where did she store the trauma of my brother's birth so she could carve out safe passage for my own? To go willingly into the belly of the beast, the beast that is your belly, is an act of faith. But to do it again and again, when you know what perils lie in wait, is a sign of great courage. She'd been lucky twice. Surely a third time was tempting fate?

How brave she must have been, to march to the threshold of life and death one last time and present the burden of her own mortality for consideration.

I never thought to ask her if she was scared. And now I will never know.

❦

Like my entry into the world, my mother's exit from it began with a yellowing of the skin, the remnants of a bruised sunset fading uneasily across the landscape of her body.

At first, we thought the cause would turn out to be relatively straightforward. We had recently spent a weekend in Sydney for my uncle's fiftieth birthday, and we thought the glow she'd assumed might have been hepatitis A, the result of some bad oysters. As far as communicable diseases go, hep A is highly treatable and is usually resolved within weeks. We laughed at the absurdity of it. My father and I were the oyster fiends and would have eaten thrice the amount my mother did. What were the odds that whatever was floating around in those shells skipped us and went straight for Luci?

The odds, as it quickly transpired, were not good.

It was the shadow that gave it away. The hospital had booked her in for a scan ('routine procedure', we were told) and the results had given her doctor some cause for concern. The shadow could turn out to be nothing—a flash of movement caught from the corner of the eye, something that could be attributed to a lack of sleep and an overactive imagination.

'But it could be something?' I asked, ever the hypochondriac.

'Let's not get ahead of ourselves,' the doctor replied. 'For now, we just want to move as quickly as possible to figure out what's going on.'

More tests were ordered. More scans. My mother was transferred from the local hospital near my parents' home to a ward at the Royal Adelaide Hospital (RAH).

I remember clearly the day we found out that the nothing we had hoped for was the something we feared. My brother and sister and I had gone to the RAH to be there when the latest results came in. We were asked to wait in the hallway, and we obeyed without protest. It was a relief to be excused from the gravity of the situation. We had arrived at the hospital as adults, but in that white ward with its white walls and white lights and white chairs, we reverted right back to childhood. As we waited, my brother and sister sat slouched on the plastic seats while I paced up and down in front of them, trying to balance as gracefully as I could on my tiptoes.

Everything is going to be okay. I repeated the mantra to myself, arms raised at my sides as I teetered along the lines on the floor like a tightrope walker.

Still, I strained to hear what was being said in the next room. I couldn't make out any of the conversation, and the face of the doctor when he emerged a few minutes later was similarly inscrutable. He scribbled something on a clipboard and then set off purposefully down the hall away from us. I heard footsteps moving towards the door of my mother's room and someone— my father, presumably—gently pushed it closed until it was only a few inches ajar.

I could hear my parents murmuring to each other, but the words were muffled. I was about to move closer to eavesdrop when my father said, '. . . and we'll just throw a big party'.

I froze, balanced on the balls of my feet in the white ward with the white walls and the white lights overlooking the white chairs. A rushing noise filled my head.

A big party. A big party. A big party.

I didn't look at my siblings, but I knew they'd heard it too. There was a static electricity in the air, and it carried with it the weight of everything we had and had not said to our mother over the course of our lives.

My arms dropped to my sides as the heels of my feet sank to the ground. I went and sat next to my sister, with whom I had exchanged various torments and unkindnesses over the years, each of us trusting that no amount of cruelty could ever be sharp enough to sever the bond that held us together; my sister, Charlotte, whose confidences I had betrayed on more than one occasion and whose suffering as the older, shyer Ford girl I had exploited rather than tried to understand; my sister, who had always forgiven me and who would continue to forgive me with grace and love for the rest of our lives.

I went to her and buried my face in her lap and I whispered, 'I'm scared.'

'Me too,' she replied.

There we were, three children sitting together and waiting as we had so many times over the years, in international airports or country bus stations or at school gates or on Christmas mornings—except this time, we were waiting to learn if our mother was going to die.

The door opened and our father appeared.

'Come in,' he said.

❦

When my mother was a child, she swallowed a fishbone while eating dinner one night. The bone lodged in her throat, and she began to choke. Her grandmother, my great-grandmother, stood up swiftly and came to her. Grabbing her plate from the table, she placed it on my mother's head and slowly began to spin it.

'Look at the plate,' she commanded.

The young girl looked up at the rim of the plate as it spun above her, her body relaxing with every passing turn. With her attention focused elsewhere, the fishbone loosened itself and slid down.

'I could have died,' my mother always said whenever she told this story. 'She saved my life.'

'Was she a witch?' I'd asked her.

'There are more things in heaven and earth, Horatio, than can be dreamt of in your philosophy,' came the cryptic answer.

When I learned the origins of this quote years later, I realised it was my mother's way of telling us to keep our minds open not just to possibility but also to magic. We cannot know what mysteries the universe holds or what it has planned for us; isn't it more fun to be open to surprises rather than insist on knowing all there is to know?

She saw the mystery in moments, my mother. Long before she became unwell, when mortality was a destination far away over a distant hill, she'd describe the magical plans she and my father had made for their shuffle off the mortal coil. When they began to lose their faculties, or had just decided they'd had enough, they'd go to a clifftop overlooking the ocean at sunset. They'd take an excess of sleeping pills with a shared bottle of wine and then, holding hands, they'd drift away together as the sun sank below the horizon one last time.

My mother had redefined her relationship with God long before this. Confirmed as a child in the Catholic Church, she'd abandoned formal religion as a young woman. She said she preferred to commune with God, or her sense of 'God', in her garden. Nurturing new life, tilling the soil, speaking to the trees—these were the things that fed her spirit.

But she also had faith in the power of stories, and one of her favourites was the dystopian science fiction film, *Blade Runner*, in which ex-policeman Rick Deckard (played by Harrison Ford) is charged with exterminating a group of replicants. The replicants are synthetic humanoids who were designed to work as slaves on planetary colonies but who have rebelled against the system and returned to earth. It's a film about power and corruption, the nature of humanity and the murky line between good and evil.

One of the final scenes is a showdown between Deckard and Roy Batty (Rutger Hauer), the leader of the replicants. The replicants were designed with a four-year lifespan, and Roy is quickly approaching the end of his. The pair engage in a dramatic chase that culminates in Deckard hanging precariously from the edge of a rooftop. Despite knowing it might hasten his own death, Roy—the supposedly artificial human—pulls his nemesis to safety. Facing Deckard, Roy delivers this potent monologue on his impending demise: *'I've seen things you people wouldn't believe. Attack ships on fire off the shoulder of Orion. I watched C-beams glitter in the dark near the Tannhäuser Gate. All those moments will be lost in time, like tears in rain. Time to die.'*

My mother loved that speech. She'd sometimes recite it, every part of her body and every inflection in her voice leaning into the performance. She had always been the most enthusiastic among her friends whenever they played charades after a boozy dinner party. But this monologue in particular was like a prayer to her. This was where she and my father would go after they drifted into the lightness of an everlasting sleep, she'd say—to the shoulder of Orion, where they would spend eternity watching the starships burn.

Rutger Hauer famously modified the original script of his character's monologue, scaling it back and removing what he called some of the 'opera talk' and 'hi-tech speech'. In an interview given after the film's release, he explained that Roy 'wanted to make his mark on existence'.

Isn't that what we all want? To know that some part of us lives on, long after the vessel of our body has burned out?

❣

At our father's invitation, my siblings and I peeled our limbs from the greasy plastic of the hospital chairs and approached the room in which our mother lay in stasis, caught at the crossroads of life and death. I didn't want to pass that threshold and hear whatever it was they had to say. I wanted to turn and run through the hall, take the stairs down to the hospital's entrance two at a time and flee this morbid site of uncertainty. I had never been a runner, but I pictured myself bursting through the front doors and sprinting as far as possible from the news I knew was coming.

Instead, I followed my brother and sister inside.

My mother was lying in bed in her cornflower blue dressing-gown, a familiar garment throughout our childhood. We made awkward small talk for a few minutes (*Are you comfortable? Is the hospital food okay? It's lucky you don't have to share a room!*), but the pretence at normality was mercifully brief. Now that we were here, it seemed better to know than not know.

'So,' my brother started, 'what's the verdict?'

'It's cancer,' my dad replied, in an even tone.

'It's in my bile duct,' my mother added, 'which explains the jaundice.'

'But they can fix it, right?' I asked.

'The outlook is pretty good,' my father replied. 'It came up on the scan, but the doctors are reasonably confident they can get it out in surgery.'

'And then what will happen?' I asked.

'Well,' my mother said, 'afterwards, we'll look at doing chemotherapy or radiation. Apparently they have very good options for chemo these days, so I might not even lose my hair!'

A question hung heavy in the room, but none of us could bring ourselves to voice it.

Are you going to die?

Instead, we posed less serious variations. *Can they get rid of it? Are the doctors optimistic?*

My parents responded vaguely. Hope for the best, prepare for the worst, that's what the doctors say. There's an increasing success rate with this kind of thing, they say. Some of their patients are still going after ten or twelve years!

Which is it? I wanted to ask. *Ten or twelve?*

Despite the injection of optimism, the heaviness remained. *Look for the tell*, my mother had said when they'd taught us to play poker. And so I looked at my father. His face was neutral as he leaned against the wall, but I noticed his hands were fidgeting. As he spoke about all the possible treatments, his fists clenched and unclenched, nails digging into his palms.

He was afraid.

I made a decision in that moment. If my father was scared, then to ease his burden I should try to be strong. I unzipped the self that I was when I entered the hospital and let it drop to the floor, quietly kicking it beneath the bed and out of sight. In its place, I slipped into something lighter and more resilient: the competent version of myself that I'd always wanted to be but had never had cause to become.

I like to think I've always been quite practical in a crisis, holding it together even as the world around me falls apart. Perhaps I respond to the theatrical aspects inherent in such scenes. There is a strength in being able to observe from a distance, to behave in a disaster as though playing a character guided by a predetermined script and structure. If I can imagine I'm performing in a play or a movie, I can determine what the end looks like. I knew I could nail this role.

And so in my mother's room that day, I prepared for my close-up.

CANCER BATTLE is the story of a dysfunctional family forced to overcome their petty differences and historical grievances when the matriarch is diagnosed with cancer. CLEMENTINE is a twenty-five-year-old hypochondriac and aspiring writer drifting between various temping jobs and working on her blog. Previously selfish, immature and irresponsible, the shock of her mother's diagnosis forces her to grow up rapidly.

I assumed the character as we left the hospital that afternoon. I said goodbye to my father on North Terrace and began to walk towards King William Street. I was thinking about stopping in at the Exeter for a drink, because having a stiff drink seemed like exactly the sort of thing the stoic protagonist would do at the end of the first sequence of *Cancer Battle*.

As I passed the bus stop, a trio of young men appeared. They were waving a camera around and pointing it at random strangers, staging the kind of obnoxious prank that would later become routine for young, chronically unfunny men looking to establish themselves as online edgelords. I steeled myself to ignore them as I walked past, a muscular instinct all young women learn when our bodies suddenly shift into being considered 'public property'.

Flash! the camera went. And again, twice more. *Flash! Flash!*

The third flash triggered something in me and I whipped around.

'Could you actually fucking not?' I snapped at them. 'I've just had some very bad news at the hospital. My mother has been diagnosed with *cancer*, for fuck's sake, and I really don't need your *shit* right now.'

It's hard to say which had a greater effect on them: the word 'cancer' (unsexy) or the sight of a woman losing her temper (deeply unsexy). Either way, they recoiled from me. I glared at them, set my face into the mask of someone who had received Very Bad News (which I had! I wasn't lying!) and headed towards the pub.

My mother has cancer, I said to myself as I made my way to the Exeter, the beer-soaked pub I'd been frequenting since my university days, mentally preparing for the mic-drop moment I would get to say those words to someone else. Even when grief and fear are abundant, there is also an undercurrent of excitement that exists within tragedy, like breathlessly reporting the news of a friend's terrible break-up or interrupting a torrential flood of tears in order to stand in front of the mirror and watch yourself cry.

It's bad news I'm afraid, I'd say to the imaginary friend I now pictured standing next to me at the bar. *It's cancer.* To punctuate the gravity of my announcement, I would shake my head in disbelief.

They'd gasp in shock and reach out a hand to place on my shoulder. *You go sit down*, they'd command. *I'll get you a drink.*

Thank you, I'd reply, world weary and heavy now that mortality had made itself known to me.

I'd sit at a table while they ordered a carafe of house wine— wait, no, let's make it a bottle of shiraz (moderately priced, let's not go crazy)—where I'd be suddenly joined by more friends.

What's happened?! they'd ask, finding the haunted look in my eyes frightening and yet strangely attractive.

My mother, I'd reply gravely. *She has cancer.*

I'd refuse to whisper the last word, and the stoicism would force them to consider me with sudden admiration. Already, there was a division between them and me. What would they cry about later that night? Boys? Girls? A bad date? Those things were insignificant to me now. My mother has *cancer,* for goodness sake—I have no time for the trivial concerns of youth!

But wait, my brain said, interrupting the fantasy. Let's try a different scenario.

My mother, I'd reply gravely. *She has cancer.*

And then I'd light a cigarette and take a deep drag, as if mocking Death and all his vainglorious conceit. *Well, I doubt this has anything to do with it!* I'd joke as they looked on, awestruck by the chic nihilism required to laugh at a time like this.

They'd shower me with sympathy, and praise me for being so strong. *You're coping so well with the situation,* I could hear one say. *I would be a* mess *if my mum were dying,* said another— something actual people really would go on to say a few months down the track, making you feel as if somehow the relationship they had with their mother was more profound than the one you had with yours; as if your apparent ability to function like a normal human being was because you just weren't as sad about the situation as they would be, because they would be a *mess,* just an absolute *mess.* But I was still in the imaginary conversation at this point, and so I reminded them that *no, actually, she's* not *dying, because the prognosis is very good and the doctors have caught it early, at least we think they have, and you know we really do have one of the best health systems in the world.* And now I was angry at the imaginary friends sitting with me in the beer-soaked pub in my head; the people I thought were regarding me with sympathy when it was actually just pity. I decided I didn't want to talk to them anymore, because they just didn't get it, and I was realising that this was probably the way it was going to be from now on: that some people were just not going to *get it*. So I told the imaginary friends that it was *fine*, that I was fine, that I wasn't worried, that the surgery was going to work and my mother was going to beat this thing because who died of cancer these days *with this health system* and *with this economy* and what did any of them know about it anyway?

I reached the door of the Exeter thoroughly put out and angry, as if the scene I'd imagined were real.

My mother has cancer, I thought to myself. *But it's all going to be completely fine.*

Entering the beer garden, I saw a friend enjoying a drink in the afternoon sun.

'Clem!' she called out cheerily as I walked towards her. 'What's up?'

I promptly burst into tears. Because as it turns out, what was up was that my mother had cancer and my God my God my God.

My mother might die.

❣

A memory. She sits at the kitchen table, wrapped in her corn-flower blue dressing-gown and clutching a mug of strong black coffee in her right hand. With her left, she brings a cigarette to her lips and takes a long drag. We're in the old house, so I cannot be more than eight years old. It's the afternoon, and she has just woken up.

'Mum?' I call to her tentatively.

'Mmmm?' she replies, only half paying attention.

'I hate you,' I whisper.

In this moment, I do not hate my mother. I love her fiercely and protectively, as I will do every day for the rest of my life, even the days when I *do* truly believe I hate her. But I have been overwhelmed by the urge to say something wicked. It strikes me abruptly, like a kind of mental dare—the same way I will later feel an urge to yell out during a theatre production or to deliberately drop a pile of plates on the floor while working as a waitress or push a stranger in front of a car. I utter the words to see what will happen and instantly want to retract them; to pull them back through the air before they reach her ears and heart and shovel them back into my cursed mouth.

My mother looks at me in surprise, her expression wounded. She says, 'Well . . . sometimes I hate you too.'

Her frank response is a revelation. It makes me realise that my mother has a life outside of me. Later, I will understand that it also means she has dreams that don't include me—dreams that will probably never come true *because* of me. It's a small glimpse of what a sacrifice motherhood can be, and I feel all the more guilty for what I've said. I run to her, bury my face in her warm chest and beg forgiveness. She soothes me as she always has and as I believe she always will, neither of us yet knowing how much of a strain adolescence will place on our relationship.

Another memory. I'm thirteen years old, prickly and suddenly secretive. I speak to my mother spitefully, eyes glazing over whenever she opens her mouth. I am twice as old as I was when I first told her I hated her, but these days I feel less guilty for saying it and less concerned about making it up to her. I take pride in hiding everything from her: the smell of cigarettes in my hair and alcohol on my breath; the diary into which I pour my self-loathing; the make-up I carry in my bag and which she says I'm too young for; the dangerous flirtation I have with an adult man I work for, a man who has recognised that I am desperate to be treated like an adult and so confides his secrets to me in the hope I might agree to become one of them too; the way I vomit my food up after every tiny meal I allow myself to eat; the fear that I might be going crazy. I hide everything from her except the withering scorn that seeps out of me whenever she looks my way.

One morning, as I'm leaving for school, she reminds me to put on my coat. It's a heavy jacket with a waxed outer layer to repel the rain, hideous and oily to the touch. I hate it and refuse to wear it, telling her my jumper will be *fine*.

She comes and stands in front of me. I'm already taller than her; I have my father's height. 'Just put it on,' she orders, tired of the constant arguments.

'Oh my *God*, Mum,' I snap at her, rolling my eyes dramatically. 'Stop being so *annoying*.'

Smack! Smack!

The hand comes out of nowhere, palm connecting with my cheek with a fierce sting.

I look at her in horror and the face that stares back at me flashes with fury.

'I cannot *stand* you right now!' she spits at me. 'What have I done to you, to make you treat me with such *disrespect*? You think I don't know what it's like to be a teenager? You're not that interesting!'

The words cut me like a knife, hot shame pouring into me where blood would otherwise be pouring out. Trying to hurt or deride my mother had become like a sport to me, and she'd finally expelled me from the match. The pain I felt over that would stay with me long after the red print of her hand had faded from my cheek.

These days, I see so much of myself in her reaction. When I was at my worst, she used to tell me that she couldn't wait for me to have children so I would finally understand what it felt like to be her. Like a curse from a fairy tale, it finally caught up with me: I had a child, and I began to understand that the most powerful forms of love and hatred can co-exist in ways we can't possibly predict.

I often feel that my love for my son is as infinite as the universe, ever expanding. But there's another side to that love, and I am deeply afraid of the darkness that lives there. The white-hot rage that's always been a part of me has become more pronounced since I became a mother. The fury I've felt when he's refused to go to sleep unless every inch of his body is touching mine. The times I've slammed plastic plates and bottles down on counters, the hardest part of my heart *wanting* my son to know that I'm slamming them down because of him, because of what *he's done to me*. Those terrible, terrifying moments when he was a baby and I had to put him down and step away to stop myself from making *him* the thing I wanted to slam onto a counter or throw against the wall, the last vestige of sanity drowning under the weight of the tedium of screams (his) and tears (mine) and sometimes vice versa. I know there will come a day when he looks at me the way I looked at my mother, with derision and scorn and, perhaps worst of all, a burning indifference to my existence. And I will both deserve it and not deserve it. This is the endless paradox of the mother–child bond. Love and hate, two sides of the same soul.

Years later, when we had become friends again, my mother told me how desperately alone she'd felt during those few years living on the farm and raising three children essentially by herself. She described the kitchen cupboards as having dents and splinters from the countless times she stood there, 'kicking the shit out of them'. More recently, I learned from my aunt that there were some mornings when she'd stay in bed for hours, leaving us to either cry in our cots or figure out how to entertain ourselves while we waited for her to come. Maybe this explains how, as an adult, I can long for someone's love and at the same time feel so disgusted when it is given to me too freely.

We consider hatred to be the prerogative of children. Angry words spat at parents are dismissed as being a natural part of youth. But now that I am a mother myself—and, more importantly, a woman with hopes and dreams and a rich interior landscape—I can finally hear what my mother was saying that day decades ago, when she was pulled out of a thought or a memory or a wistful daydream by a child who was beginning to test her boundaries. This is a message sent through time—thirty years of it, in fact. A warning, but also a recognition: *Motherhood can so often feel like a prison, with rage the only means of escape.*

As a child and then a teenager, I thought the battleground of feelings, recriminations and blame were mine alone. But I understand now there were times when my mother hated me too—moments when all mothers must hate their children— fiercely and passionately and for reasons far more complex than I was able to then comprehend. For my mother, this hatred had no outlet or voice. Like so many of us, she was seen as a mother first, a wife second and a woman last.

Mothers belong to everyone but themselves, and they are not allowed to view their children as anchors that have the power to drag them under.

❣

The surgery was scheduled for the following week. We approached the date with a mixture of excitement and trepidation, still clinging to the view that the outlook was positive. The doctors seemed confident that the tumour was isolated to the bile duct and liver, and removing it would be fairly straightforward. The tumour's location was a blessing; the liver is the only internal human organ that can regenerate itself, and it can be sectioned by up to three-quarters with no lasting damage. It seemed like a good portent, and we reminded each other of that whenever we discussed the potential for unwelcome surprises.

There would be recovery time, of course; six weeks of bed rest followed by radiation and chemotherapy. But these were the normal hallmarks of cancer treatment, and people survived cancer all the time, my family and I reassured each other.

It would all be fine, I thought to myself. I'd suffered the usual slings and arrows of adolescence and self-indulgent torment, but nothing truly terrible had ever happened to me. It didn't seem possible that this thing, this shadow, this ticking time bomb growing deep within my mother could really be powerful enough to blast a hole through my entire world.

I remember the day of the surgery well. It was late October; summer had almost arrived, but the evening air was still brisk. I was sitting outside the Exeter drinking wine and smoking cigarettes with my friend Laura when the phone rang.

Dad Mobile the flashing screen announced.

I answered, surprised to be hearing from him so soon. The operation was expected to take around six hours, but barely two hours had passed since she'd gone into theatre.

'Dad?' I said. 'What's wrong? Why are you calling me so early?'

The response was a sound unlike anything I'd ever heard from my father before. I can only describe it as a howl of unfettered grief.

'Is Mum okay?' I asked.

'*No*,' he answered, and it was less a word than a keening moan.

What the doctors hadn't been able to detect with their scans and fancy equipment became apparent the moment they opened her up and took a look inside. Tumours. Tumours everywhere, a wasteland of tumours. *Keep out.*

They closed her up again. *We're sorry*, they said. *There was nothing we could do. It was worse than we thought.* Perhaps they went home to their families, hugged their partners and children more tightly than usual, reminded once more of the fragile nature of life. But then again, maybe they were accustomed to working alongside death. Maybe it no longer shocked them, because there would always be more disease and more people who believed their despair and fear were powerful enough to safeguard them from it.

And love too. We had made the mistake of thinking love would be enough. No one loved my mother more than my father. It had been mythologised throughout the years, related over countless dinner tables. Like our birth stories, we always delighted in hearing him tell the tale of the man who took up a collection one night in a British pub because he overheard the beautiful young barmaid who worked there telling her boss that her bag had been stolen while she was in a phone box calling her sister to say she was on her way home.

'I'm going to marry that woman,' he'd told his friends when she first appeared, and they all laughed because it was well known that she didn't go out with anyone, least of all giant, hairy roughnecks with broad Australian accents.

But when he presented her with the imperial pint glass filled with coins and notes and asked her to go to dinner with him, she said yes. *Why? Why did you say yes?!* we always demanded, as if we hadn't heard the story a million times before.

'Because he made me laugh,' she'd reply, while my father looked into his wine glass and smiled, as if he still couldn't believe his luck.

Crying outside the pub that night, I grieved for a thousand things. For my father, who had shown his love for my mother by making things for her: a decorative water pitcher with pink bougainvillea flowers frozen into the casing; a portable shower for when we went camping on the beach; a life. I grieved for my mother, who had yet to emerge from the fog of anaesthesia and so didn't know that her expiration date had moved sharply into focus. I thought of her there in the hospital, with its cold lighting and uncomfortable beds, waiting to hear that this was it, she had reached the end, do not pass go, do not collect $200. I grieved for all the things she hadn't yet done, the injustices and traumas she'd suffered throughout her life, the places she wouldn't get to see again or to visit for the first time, the well-thumbed books she loved and returned to over and over that would now sit unread, the resonance of particular passages lost to time just like the passage of her life itself.

And I grieved for me. Because I was still a child, *her* child, and I always would be. But there would soon come a time when I could no longer reach out and touch her, or bury my face in her shoulder and smell the soft creaminess of her skin—the first scent I had ever known—or listen to the steady rhythm of her heartbeat, which had soothed me before I even knew what time or consciousness were. My mother was going to die, and her death was going to leave me unmoored in some essential way that could never be reclaimed or corrected. She was the blueprint to my entire existence. What would I do without her?

It is not loss that we feel when we have our mothers taken from us. In a 2016 article in *The Guardian*, writer David Ferguson described the reality as being far more violent than that. It is an un-mothering that 'feels raw and fundamental, a pain that reaches all the way down to your ligaments and bones'.

Before we are born, we swirl in the cocoon of that space in our mother's womb. As Ferguson put it so eloquently, they are 'our first firmament, literally, our first homes, the universe from whose substance we were formed'.

My first home was a soft meadow whose lush ground had nurtured life at the very beginning of its creation, but the meadow was now riddled with landmines. Before too long, they were going to start exploding. The meadow would be laid to waste, all that it had nourished there left starved in some way, and I could do nothing but watch as it happened.

❣

My mother came home from the hospital and we began her treatment program in earnest. When I say 'we', I mean 'I'. And when I say 'treatment program', I mean 'researching every bit of wellness gobbledegook you can find on the internet and ordering grossly expensive miracle cures'. I took some time off work and moved home temporarily, throwing away all the packets of cigarettes my mother had stockpiled in the drawers and replacing them with vitamins. I talked my dad into buying a juicer, because some people consider daily glasses of fresh vegetable juice, gentle walks and mindfulness to be the secret cancer cure Big Pharma is trying to stop us from discovering.

'You should try meditating,' I said to my mother. 'And we should start walking every day. Here, have some carrot juice.'

I sent away for an expensive powdered tea from Canada because it purported to 'detoxify' the body and break down cancerous tumours, flushing them out with the rest of our daily waste—and it smelled bad enough for that to be true. I diligently brewed it for her every day, leaving it to steep while she drank the glass of freshly crushed carrots, celery, spinach and apples that I'd fed through the juicer and then supervising closely as she drained the cup of expensive bog water. We spent the rest of our mornings drinking cups of tea on the small deck at the house my parents had lovingly renovated together, talking about this and that while steering clear of the growing elephant in the room.

At noon, we'd choose between the midday movie or an episode of *Oprah* (who my mother always incomprehensibly referred to as 'Off-rah'). She'd provide a running commentary of whatever was happening on screen, verbally nudging me to respond as I gritted my teeth in irritation next to her. Back then, not even rapidly approaching death was compelling enough to have me relax my stance on Television Talkers.

I sometimes went out in the evenings, catching the train back into the city and staying the night in the house I shared with three other women on the southern fringe of Adelaide. I went to the pub with friends, drinking wine and smoking cigarettes and talking about anything other than what was going on. I was sick of people asking me the same questions all the time, and I was sick of never having a different answer to offer them.

'How's your mum?' they'd ask, a careful note of concern in their voices.

'Yeah, fine, doing well,' I'd reply, trying to ignore the worried looks that passed between them.

What more could I say?

The thing is, she *did* seem to be doing well. The surgery hadn't been the cure-all we'd hoped for, but the radiation treatment she'd started was actually making her feel a little better. The sickly yellow of the jaundice had faded from her skin, and her cheeks had turned a rosy pink. She was sometimes able to stomach a few sips of wine, and these were the nights when she laughed the most. In this jovial state, with a spring in her step and a healthy glow about her, it was difficult to believe in the disease that was tearing her insides apart. We allowed ourselves to imagine that it wasn't as bad as they'd thought. That perhaps we would get those years after all—ten or twelve, it didn't matter; either would do.

I was so confident in her improvement that I booked a holiday to Cairns with my boyfriend. Before we left though, my mother developed a fever and went into hospital as a precaution. I wanted to cancel my trip, but she said not to be silly.

'I don't want you to miss out on things because of this,' she said. 'I'll be fine, and you'll only be gone for a week.'

I spent the next few days swimming in waterholes, driving past burnt golden sugarcane fields and trying not to feel guilty about how much lighter I felt. The truth is that it was a relief to be away from the impending shadow of grief, and I threw myself into all the things that make being alive feel so good: nature, food, laughter and sex. We were on a dive boat on the Great Barrier Reef when my father called the emergency number I'd left with him. The fever had grown progressively worse over the last couple of days, with no sign of it breaking.

'What are you telling me?' I asked, my hand gripping the satellite phone tightly, the softness gone from my muscles and replaced by the now-familiar tension of fear.

'You need to come home now if you want to say goodbye,' he replied.

As mercy dashes go, this one was reasonably dramatic. We paid an extraordinary amount of money to be conveyed from the boat to shore by helicopter, then raced to the airport. I was just beginning to panic about the distance we still had to travel when my father called again, this time with good news. The fever had broken, and my mother had woken up weak but still wonderfully, gloriously alive. A reprieve.

My father had said we wouldn't need to come to the hospital until the following morning, and so we spent the next two hours waiting for our flight in the airport bar and getting deliriously drunk. When we finally landed, I went home and passed out in a stupor, exhausted from the tears and the wine and the seemingly endless rollercoaster ride that cancer had shown itself to be.

The next morning, I found my mother sitting up against her pillows and looking very much not like a woman who had almost died the night before. I rushed to her side and buried my head in her chest, breathing in the scent that was more familiar to me than my own skin.

'I wish you hadn't come back,' she said, stroking my hair. 'I feel terrible that you cut your trip short!'

'Don't be ridiculous,' I replied, holding on to her tightly. 'I shouldn't have gone in the first place.'

New scans revealed an inflammation in her stomach that wasn't responding to treatment. She was transferred to the Calvary North Adelaide Hospital, where she spent a week, and then another week. I had gone back to work by this point, burying myself in a project I was coordinating so that I could avoid thinking about the sand that was rapidly hurtling towards the bottom of the hourglass. It had been days since I'd seen her or even spoken to her. I told myself it was because I was so busy, but really I was battling the unspoken eighth stage of grief—the malaise of waiting for an inevitable death to finally arrive.

I had just finished work for the day when she called me. I answered chirpily, saying hello and asking her how she was, trying to quell the guilt that was already creeping in.

Her voice was small and hesitant on the phone. 'Clementine? Will you come and visit me, please?'

The shame. Oh, the shame I still feel.

Inside me there is a universe of regret, containing galaxies of things I did and did not do over the course of my life with my mother, my mirror. This remains the worst phone call I've ever had in my life, worse even than the one in which my father howled in anguish down the line. I had allowed the normality of my life to creep back in and had abandoned my mother to deal with the conclusion of her own by herself. I have never been able to forgive myself for this; will never forgive myself for this. Years later, after I had left my son's father and signed up to a series of dating apps, a personality test on one of them would ask me if I was able to name the worst thing I'd ever done and I would reply without hesitation: *Yes.*

I went straight to the hospital. My mother's new room was comfortable and dimly lit, but nothing covers the smell of a hospital. The thought of her spending endless days there by herself broke me.

'I'm sorry,' I said to her, my eyes filling with tears.

'It's okay,' she said, holding my hand. 'I'm glad you came.'

I sat with her and we talked, about everything and nothing. Every few minutes, she reached for one of the disposable bags that had been left beside her bed and vomited into it. There was nothing but bile in her now. Her stomach was no longer just inflamed, it had stopped working altogether. There would be no more glasses of wine drunk with exuberant dinners. She'd never again stand over the kitchen counter spreading real butter onto fresh bread, no more eating mangoes over the sink, the sweet juice dripping down her arms, no more slathering chilli oil over a slice of pizza in the way she liked. She had been fastidious about tea, never letting any of us make it for her because she always insisted she could taste how badly we timed the brew. Over the years, we had joked that she'd be late to her own funeral because she wanted 'just one more cup'. Watching her that day filling the plastic bags with the remains of her insides reminded me that she'd never drink tea again, and the denial of this simple pleasure seemed to me to be one of the cruellest things of all.

At some point, one of her doctors arrived to update her on their treatment plan. I listened carefully, trying to assume a facade of maturity and level-headedness. I wanted to be the buffer between her and whatever terrible news was to be delivered next in the series of terrible news that had punctuated the last eight months. I failed, of course, because the terrible news made real and tangible something I'd been trying for so long to pretend wasn't happening—because how *could* it really, actually, finally happen?

The doctor explained that because my mother's digestive system had stopped working, she couldn't keep any food or liquids down. This explained the constant retching. She was, in essence, starving. Their last remaining option was to perform a gastric bypass procedure. It would buy her three months, maybe four.

She absorbed this information calmly. What else can you do?

When the doctor had left, my mother asked if I wanted to take a stroll to the hospital chapel. I offered her my arm for support as we walked there. The chapel was quiet and peaceful, and I remember that we were the only people in the room—a room that had surely seen many bargains offered and recriminations screamed. We sat in one of the wooden pews and I began to cry, heaving, racking sobs.

'*Shhhh*,' my mother soothed me. '*Shhhhhh.*'

She pulled my head down into her lap and began to stroke my hair, as she must have done so many times when I was a baby and then a small child keening for her, as she must have wanted to do so many times when I was a snarly adolescent pushing her away.

'It isn't fair!' I howled into her lap.

'No,' she agreed. 'But who deserves fair?'

She continued to stroke my hair until my tears subsided, her fingers combing through the long tresses. When I was younger, she'd always warned me against doing anything 'too drastic' to it.

'There are women who'd kill for hair like yours,' she'd tell me. Which, to be fair, also seems a little drastic, when you think about it.

When I was seventeen, I went to the hairdresser in the strip mall around the corner and handed them a photograph of Drew Barrymore that I'd snipped out of *Dolly* or *Girlfriend*. Her bleached hair had been cropped into a pixie cut and decorated with daisies, a very 'of the nineties' look that I was desperate to replicate. My mother—from whom I'd hidden the appointment—was *appalled* when I came home.

'Why would you *do* this to yourself?' she demanded, destroying the last semblance of false bravado I'd mustered in the hairdresser's chair while looking at the disastrous results.

It took me a long time to grow out that regrettable haircut, but more would follow. Here, though, in the chapel, it was exactly the way she'd always liked it. I breathed more evenly into her lap as she continued to soothe me.

After a time, she spoke. 'Bad things happen all the time to people who want to believe they don't deserve it,' she told me in a soft voice. 'You can go outside and shake your fist at the night sky, screaming to God or whatever or whoever you believe in, "Why me?! Why us?!"'

She paused. My head was still in her lap, and my hands clutched at the fabric of her dressing-gown.

'But if you wait for the answer,' she continued, 'if you listen *hard enough*, you'll hear a voice answering through the dark.

"Why not you?"'

❤

I left my mother's hospital room that night feeling defeated and grief-stricken, but inside I had already begun to accept the inevitability of what we were facing. We had three or four months. And even though it was nothing, it was also *something*.

My mother wanted to spend some time at home before she had to deal with another surgery, so the next day my father went to pick her up. I spoke to her on the phone that night, and she seemed to be in fine spirits. She asked me to fill her in on the celebrity gossip that she knew I consumed religiously. For a period of time throughout her illness, I'd been buying her copies of the tabloids my friends and I passed between us at uni. One day, shortly before her latest hospital stint, she suddenly tossed aside her magazine, abandoning the story she'd been reading about Britney Spears or Jennifer Aniston, or possibly even both of them.

'I can't read this rubbish anymore,' she said. What had been a distraction from her prognosis had morphed into a flippant mockery of it. I stopped bringing her magazines after that, but she occasionally humoured my chatter about articles I'd read. That night, I told her all about Lindsay Lohan's alcohol addiction and how Alec Baldwin had yelled at his daughter on a voicemail.

'Goodnight, Mummy,' I said.

'Goodnight, darling,' she replied.

Her surgery was scheduled for a few days' time, but my father had invited us all home that weekend to have dinner for Mother's

Day. I had missed the train, so by the time I arrived I was an hour late.

'Hello!' I called out as I walked into the kitchen, pouring myself a glass of wine and trying to ignore my father's look of irritation. My mother sat in the corner quietly, her face fixed in an expression I couldn't quite make out.

We chatted for a bit, my siblings and I picking at some of the nibbles my father had laid out. Before too long, he interrupted us. 'Well,' he said, 'we have some news for you.'

I could tell by his tone that the 'news', whatever it was, wasn't good. The pretence at light-heartedness was immediately dispelled. I gripped the stem of my glass tightly, my cheeks grown hot from impending panic.

'What's going on?' I asked.

There was no cushioning the blow. Instead, my father got straight to the point.

'Your mother has decided not to have the operation,' he told us. 'She's ready to go.'

The room grew still.

'What does that mean, "ready to go"?' I asked after a moment.

My mother had been sitting stony-faced, in what I now recognise was steely resolve. She looked up and told us how she had come to her decision. She didn't want to spend more time in hospital, or have to endure all the pain and suffering the operation would entail, just to prolong the inevitable.

'They expect it will be quick,' she told us, as if this would somehow lessen the pain of the very worst thing that could ever happen to any of us. The three or four months I had been banking on disappeared. We were talking about a matter of days.

Then my father spoke the words that have been seared across my soul forevermore.

'We've asked you here tonight to say goodbye.'

We looked at him, tears beginning to stream down our faces. *What?*

'After tonight, you'll go home,' he told us. 'She doesn't want any of you to come back. And we'll . . . well, we'll stay here and wait.'

The blood that had filled my cheeks before rushed with full force into my skull, the roar of it drowning out the rest of my father's words. I stumbled outside and lay on the ground, every memory of every touch, every kiss, every argument and every shared laugh surging up through me and crashing out in wet, howling sobs. Say goodbye? How could I be ready to say goodbye?

I cried and I cried and I cried, and as I stared at the night sky an explosion of anger went off inside me. *How dare you!* I said to the universe. *Why? Why would you do this to us?*

But after a moment, there it was. The voice that my mother had told me about, the one that travels through the darkness to whisper in your ear.

Why not you?

Why not us, indeed?

Shortly after, my sister came out to sit beside me on the ground. She was crying too, and we held each other in our grief for a few minutes before going back inside.

I don't remember what we ate for dinner that night. I can't imagine there was much conversation. The only thing worth talking about was the one thing none of us wanted to acknowledge. But eventually, the time came to do what my mother had asked of us—to say goodbye.

I had always planned to stay over and go home the next morning, and I watched as Charlotte hugged our mother, crying and not wanting to let go. My mother was inscrutable, holding her but maintaining the frustratingly calm exterior she'd worn all night. It was only when my brother turned to leave after his own farewell that I saw the mask slip. I suppose she hadn't realised I was watching her so closely, but when he stepped out the door I saw it. Her forehead crumpling, her fingers brushing against her lips before reaching out to them, wanting to call them both back and hold on to them for as long as she might be allowed.

It took me a long time to process the anger I felt about my mother rejecting a treatment that might have kept her with us longer. Time promises us nothing but the world, and we selfishly, greedily always want more of it. I resented my brother in particular for having her tears. She'd always treated him differently from us girls—more tenderly, I felt, and with softer hands. I cried watching her say goodbye to him, but I felt jealous too, and the feeling stuck with me. The mask had returned when I said my own goodbye the next morning. Even when I turned to run back for a second chance, she remained stoic in her resolve, simply pushing me gently away from her and saying, 'Go now.'

For years, I thought of her decision in terms of myself. How her death impacted *me*. How *I* felt when she'd asked us to walk away. What it meant for *us* to have her go. Now that I'm a mother myself, I realise what a huge test of will it must have been for *her* to say goodbye to her children. To wear that mask not just to protect us from her suffering, but to protect herself from the temptation to reverse the decision she'd made. She didn't want us to watch her die, and she didn't want us to be the ones to make her stay. It was that simple.

Years earlier, on three separate occasions, she had walked bravely into the mystery to claim the children who were hers. Now, at the end of her life, she was being called back.

She was ready. She knew the way.

❣

Luciana Rosetta Gouveia died in the early hours of 16 May 2007. My father called that morning, and in a calm voice told me that my mother had 'begun her long and final journey to Orion'.

This is where we imagine her now, on the shoulder, watching the starships burn, just as she always said she would. Sometimes, I stand outside and look up at the constellation, talking to her and telling her about my day. She would be proud of me, I think, if not always approving of my methods. She would have loved the writers' festivals I'd have been able to take her to; would have been shy at first around the authors she admired but then would've charmed them with her wit and intelligence.

I'm not sure what she would have made of the changing world. She was fifty-eight when she died, an age that manages to be both old and young, depending on the angle from which you look at it. Old enough to have lived a relatively full life. Young enough to strike fear into the hearts of others staring down the barrel of inevitable mortality.

When I was a child, I remember conceiving of my mother's age in relation to that of other adults I knew. She was invariably always a few years older than the mothers of my friends, and the fact of that always unsettled me. *My mother?* I'd say, whenever the topic of parental age came up, which it did with surprising frequency. *She was really old when she had my sister*, I'd offer by way of explanation. *Almost twenty-nine.*

Now, when I hear about women getting married and having babies in their twenties, I cannot help but gasp and involuntarily raise a hand to my chest. *Too young!* I protest.

I remember the afternoon of her funeral well. My father had explicitly requested that no family beyond our immediate circle be present, with the exception of his own mother. We huddled together, the five of us, in the expansively large funeral home my father had chosen for the service and then cremation. When I arrived, he was visiting with her body (because this was all that remained of her now, her body) in the viewing room off to the side of the entrance. When he eventually emerged, he invited us to come in and see her.

To my surprise, I flinched on rounding the corner and seeing my mother's still, waxen face. I hadn't been prepared for what the body might look like in the coffin, but fear soon gave way to curiosity and I crept towards her like a small child. My father had arranged for her to be buried in a smart linen suit, a favourite of hers that she hadn't been able to fit into for some years now, since long before cancer ravaged her insides. Despite my grief, I couldn't help but smile wryly at the thought she'd achieved her goal weight at last.

I had never seen a dead body before and I've never seen one since, but everything I'd heard turned out to be true. The dead do look like they're sleeping, but you couldn't really mistake them for being in a slumber. An essence is missing; there is no imperceptible rise and fall of a chest, no air or breath or vitality. I was both frightened and fascinated by the absence of any trace of her, and before I could stop myself I tentatively reached out a finger to poke her cheek. It was cold and hard like marble. It shocked me, and I yanked my hand back quickly as if I had been burned.

The funeral itself seemed like a strange kind of fever dream. With a dearth of guests, the service echoed throughout the room, punctuated by the weeping of the small family huddled in front. Even through the intensity of my grief at the time, I was preoccupied with the bizarre fact of having a stranger oversee the death ceremony of someone he'd never met. Why was this bespectacled man standing in front of us talking about my dead mother? Why was she in that long box in front of us, with the lid shut? And why in the ever-loving *fuck* was no one else who loved her allowed to be here?

Later, after the conveyor belt had delivered her to the incinerator and we had gone home to drink ourselves into a stupor, I lay down on my parents' bed and placed my head on her pillow. I could still smell her, even though it had been a few days since she'd died. I curled my legs until I was lying in the foetal position, but the heartbeat that would have soothed me in the swirling universe of my origin all those years before could no longer be heard. It seemed impossible that there could be more tears left in me, but there they were again, fresh and abundant. It occurred to me in a particularly final kind of way that I would never see her or touch her again, not even as a dead body. She was gone, burned down into a pile of ashes that would be given to us in an urn, which seems like a fairly insufficient vessel in which to store the remains of a woman's life.

For a brief moment, I panicked, fixated on the mother-shaped hole that had been left in my life. If I couldn't touch her or see her, where had she gone?

In the months after she died, I saw her in the strangest of places. A patch of wildflowers near my front gate, thriving against all odds in the heart of winter. A favourite song of hers playing on the radio, moments after I had been struck by the terrible pain of missing her. The sudden impulse to call her with news or gossip, having forgotten for a brief moment that she would never answer the phone again.

Sometimes it seems as if she drifts in on the breeze, the scent of her wafting underneath my nose and enveloping me like a warm hug. I can feel her nails running softly down my back, hear her voice whispering in my ear. I close my eyes and bathe in the sound and scent and essence of her, finding her in the cracks that exist between this world and the next.

Cheryl Strayed talks about the fear that lives inside those of us whose mothers died young, and the superstition that we will be next. It seems inconceivable to us that we could reach the point at which their footprints stop and be allowed to continue moving forward without them there to lead the way. But if I'm lucky, there will come a time when I surpass my mother in age; when I assume a knowledge denied to her of the creakiness of ageing bones, the frailty of a body bending closer and closer to the ground it's destined to return to. When I reach that moment, the timeline beyond her existence on earth, how will I feel? I can only hope I get to find out, bittersweet as the moment will be.

Grief is a rushing river that in time delivers us to the sea. We never escape it, but soon enough the rapids give way to gentle waves. In that great body of water, we can see that we are part of something bigger. Call it heaven, if you like. Call it the universe. Call it magic.

I choose to call it love.

❦

Recently, I found myself gently prising my son's beloved Lego catalogue out of his hands at bedtime and placing it beneath his pillow.

'This way,' I said to him, 'the stories will find their way into your dreams.'

He fixed me with a serious gaze, as if I'd told him something magical was about to happen, which of course I had. He settled his head on the pillow, clutching Teddy, and slowly drifted off to sleep. He woke up some time later—unusual for him now that we'd emerged from the hellscape months of intermittent sleep and numerous night-time awakenings. I took him to the toilet, gave him some water and closed my eyes again as he flicked through his Lego book once more. I woke the next morning to find him curled into me, his sweet face lost in a dream. Later, when I made our bed, I found the Lego catalogue tucked back under the pillow. He knew where the books went now.

The older I get, the more I long to know who my mother was. To know who we might have become together, in time, if time had been granted to us.

But in these moments with my son, I see that she is still here. That, in fact, part of what I've become is her. She goes on living in me. My son carries her with him every day, just as she carried part of him all those years ago, in the parts of me that were forming inside her.

We are all connected. The body finds a way to remember.

On an ordinary winter's morning, under the expanse of the western Queensland sky in winter, I was born yellow to a woman far away from her own home. She sat with me for the first twenty-four hours of my life, exhausted and spent, but determined to protect my eyes from the blazing light shining down on me. Soon, when the sickly yellow had given way to the customary freshness of a new baby's skin, they lifted me from the incubator and handed me to her once again, removing the bandages that had shielded her from my view.

Twice, within the first moments of my life, I opened my eyes to gaze upon the woman who had come to claim me. My mother. My first firmament. My home.

What would I say to her, if I could speak to her now?

I have always loved you.

I miss you.

I'm sorry.

May we meet again.

2

THE QUEEN OF COOL

I'm not a particularly gloomy person. I read *Wuthering Heights* and *Jane Eyre* as a teenager but, outside of tortured diary entries detailing all the ways my parents didn't understand me accompanied by crude drawings of my body that made me look like either a heavy water balloon suspended by the neck or a misshapen duck, I could never really summon the passion for a demanding routine of gothic depression. I occasionally wore black, but only because my mother had once told me it was slimming.

Sartorially, I alternated between clothes I found in op shops and those bought in places that catered mainly to middle-aged men named Gary. This meant a steadily rotating mix of polyester caftans and ill-fitting men's trousers, and occasionally (because the nineties were very big on the dress'n'pants combo) both at the same time.

I was drawn to the caftans primarily because I thought they made me seem interesting and mysterious, but also because they covered my mid-section in a way that nineties contemporary fashion simply refused to. And as much as I'd like to say my fondness for men's trousers was due to me being effortlessly cool and androgynous, I think we can all agree the existence of the caftans makes that impossible. I chose the men's trousers for two reasons. The first was that men are allowed to have girth, and they eclipsed the minimal sizing found in the fashion hellholes where women are banned from having any hips whatsoever, and possibly also a butt crack. The second was that I had formed the habit (or the habit had formed me) of avoiding wearing anything too overtly feminine, because the thought of being judged by my peers as someone who considered themselves worthy of the title of 'girl' was too humiliating.

It was an exceptionally hot look overall, largely because everything I owned was extremely flammable. Luckily, as previously stated, I was not cool enough to be part of a subculture like 'goth' or 'aspiring teen witch', so the risk of me coming too close to any candles was minimal.

I had more of an opportunity than most teenagers to experiment with my overall aesthetic, because my family moved around so often. Unfortunately for me, I wasn't the kind of 'new girl' who piques the interest of her classmates, no matter how desperately

I wished I were. To be that kind of girl, you need to be at least one of two things (and preferably both):

1. Hot
2. Cool

The combination of these two things would make you worldly, which is like reaching the summit of Mount Everest in terms of adolescent Cool Girl cache. And although I had indeed lived in enough foreign countries to be considered worldly in a technical sense, I had never kissed a boy (at least, not outside of party games of Truth or Dare, where being dared to kiss me always seemed to elicit an audible groan) or been fingered at a dance, both of which were considered essential requirements.

I knew this, yet I greeted each new social setting with naive optimism. Perhaps *this* would be the place where being a bookish nerd would be highly valued! Maybe the kids at *this* school would appreciate the back catalogue of Andrew Lloyd Webber and celebrate a girl who was happy to engage you directly on what Disney got wrong in their animated retelling of *The Hunchback of Notre Dame*!

I think you know where this is going.

❣

In 1996, my family moved from Brisbane to Adelaide. We had only moved to Australia from the UK a year earlier, and had moved to the UK two years before that from my childhood home in Oman. I had been uncool in each of these places, a fact that had become far more pronounced in Brisbane, when I'd made the questionable choice to have my long hair cut into a style that I thought was reminiscent of Gwyneth Paltrow's but in actual fact more closely resembled a member of one of the many boy bands that graced us with their same-ishness that decade.

This latest move took place in August, meaning that I was not only forced to start a new school (again), but I had to do it at the start of term four. I have no idea why my parents hated me and wanted me to be unhappy, but there it is.

My early days at Trinity College were characterised by many of the same elements that had been present at the other schools I'd attended. There was deep, crushing anxiety on my part (not to mention the bad haircut) and, from everyone else, a brief curiosity that quickly gave way to almost total indifference. By virtue of the unspoken, invisible hierarchy of power that exists across all secondary schools, I was quickly identified as a member of the Unpopulars and invited to join them forthwith. I accepted my place gratefully; at least I would have somewhere to sit at lunch.

The first Friday of term four at my new school turned out to be casual clothes day. This meant that instead of checked summer dresses and straw hats, the schoolyard would be full of girls in low-slung, bootleg jeans and t-shirts made by Roxy or Billabong. (The nineties were not a particularly good decade for fashion, which might explain why choker necklaces were so popular then but certainly doesn't explain why they're making a comeback now.)

I laboured carefully over my outfit choice, not wanting to pass up the opportunity to show my classmates the Real Me. I finally settled on my wide-leg Tencel jeans (for anyone below the age of thirty-five, Tencel is a kind of denim so soft it lacks absolutely any structure whatsoever, the material production of which has surely been partially responsible for the climate crisis we find ourselves in now), a white singlet that belonged to my mother, a cardigan in dusty rose chenille (a kind of unattractive wool that seemed to be made almost entirely out of plastic—it was one of my favourites) and my suede Adidas sneakers. It was a look that I figured would make me seem both feminine and edgy, two traits I was sure would be welcomed enthusiastically by the fifteen-year-old boys at Trinity.

It didn't work.

Still, I was thrilled when Jenny Turner turned to me in science class and said, 'Cool shoes. I guess you're kind of a Triple J person, hey?'

I nodded.

'Yeah,' I replied nonchalantly, trying to hide the glow that was beginning to burn brightly inside (and not wanting my cardigan to catch alight). 'I'm pretty into Triple J.'

She smiled at me kindly.

'Cool,' she replied, turning back to her work.

Inwardly, I heaved a sigh of relief that she hadn't asked me to list my favourite songs or artists. The truth is that, until that point, I hadn't been entirely sure whether or not 'Australia's youth station' was pronounced 'Triple J' or just J-J-J. Most of the time, I listened to old Ella Fitzgerald CDs and the original cast recording of *Les Misérables*. The only radio station I tuned into was Mix 102.3, which was the home of my two favourite programs—*Love Song Dedications* (because it made me hopeful that someone might one day dedicate a song to me) and *Dr Feelgood* (because it made me feel good in my downstairs area but also educated and prepared; one day, I hoped to have sexual intercourse, and I wanted to be ready).

When the class ended, I loitered at the door pretending to tie my shoelace, in the hope that Jenny would invite me to have lunch with her and the other cool kids on the chapel steps. But she didn't.

'See ya!' she said, giving me a little wave as she walked past.

'Bye!' I called back.

Too eager, I thought to myself. *Be cool!*

❣

My family lived in Gawler, a town about forty kilometres north of Adelaide. It was billed as the 'gateway to the Barossa', which in terms of tourism slogans is kind of like saying 'she's weird but her cousin has a pool'. I remember the day of the move clearly. It was hot and dry, the kind of day where you feel like all the moisture has been sucked from your body, leaving nothing but a brittle nest of hair and fingernails behind.

My parents had found a sandstone house at the top of a hill with a cottage out back that I made loud noises about wanting to live in (while secretly hoping to be denied the right to, because

I am and always have been scared of the dark and am comforted by the knowledge that someone is sleeping in the next room). They were busy doing Moving Things, so I volunteered to walk down to the local supermarket to pick up some groceries. It was further than I'd realised, and as I dragged the shopping bags up the seemingly endless climb of Calton Road, I abandoned all the romantic thoughts I'd had about getting a bicycle and riding to school.

'Muuuuuuuum!' I called out when I got home, still some years off from learning for myself how excruciating that wail can be. 'I'm baaaack! Where should I put the stuff?'

'In the fridge in the cottage!' she yelled back, stating what can only be described as the *fucking obvious*.

I heaved a tortured sigh in response, as if I'd been asked to trek to the top of a mountain (again!), and lumbered the literal ten metres down to the granny flat, which my parents had somewhat obscurely chosen as the location for our kitchen. I put the cold things away and left the rest of it on the counter for someone else to deal with, reasoning I had done my part. I'd practically scaled *Everest*, for god's sake. With *heavy bags*.

My brother was coming through the screen door when I went upstairs ('upstairs' being how we would come to refer to the actual house, which sat on a slight incline in relation to the cottage, making it technically higher but only by a bit).

'Watch it!' I screeched, having determined early on in life never to miss an opportunity to fight with him.

'Fuck off!' he said.

'Daaaaaaaaad!' I whined. 'Make him stop!'

'*Both of you* stop it!' Dad boomed back. The heat had not subsided, and no one was in the mood for a teenage girl with attitude. 'Clementine, go start unpacking your things!'

I stormed up to my bedroom and surveyed the scene. Boxes filled the centre of the room. My bed was pushed into the corner, and along one wall was the ugliest, most ramshackle wardrobe I'd ever seen in my life. There were numerous compartments and drawers, none of which closed properly because the cheap plyboard had warped over the years. There was a mirror in the centre, and I stood there and looked at myself for a few minutes. My face was still red from the long walk up the hill and the sweat had dried in my hair, plastering the shaggy boy band locks flat against my cheeks. I lifted my shirt and prodded my stomach, turning from side to side to assess my body from all angles.

If I could only be thin, I thought, *my life would be amazing. I'd be pretty and popular and all the boys would like me.*

It's a terrible thing, this view we have as young girls that our real lives—our *happy* lives—are sitting just over the horizon, waiting for us to become small enough to fit into them. Tiny, wispy creatures who could be carried around in someone else's pocket, like a lip gloss or a condom or an old lolly wrapper.

The funny thing is that I had been thin before. Properly thin, people-worried-about-you thin, and I hadn't experienced any of the features of what I thought constituted a good life. It hadn't made me more popular. It hadn't snared me a boyfriend.

And it certainly hadn't made me happy. Now, over a quarter of a century later, I think maybe adolescence is just supposed to suck. Ask anyone who survived the trauma of high school and lived to see who the Beautiful People became and you'll hear the same thing: nobody wants to peak when they're fifteen. But I didn't know that then, and so I looked in the mirror and continued adding to the endless mental catalogue of things I would change about myself if I could.

This was the house in which I would spend the remainder of my adolescence. This was the bedroom where my goals and ambitions would be formed, and in which I would perfect the art of masturbating very, very quietly. This was the mirror that would witness it all, that would see every discernible angle of my body, the outfits pulled on and torn off, the tears, the posturing, the puckering of lips and the deeply private forays into imagining what it would be like to 'make my body move sexy'. Over the next few years, the bedroom would come to know all my secrets, held tight to my chest at night or breathed down the phone after I had dragged it into my room on its long extension cord. Sometimes, it would be privy to the secrets of other girls too; girls who'd come to eat candied popcorn and watch movies and squawk late into the night before quietly speaking the name of their crushes into the dark and then commanding in a giggling whisper: 'Don't tell *anyone*, you have to promise!'

'*I never would*,' was always the reply, fingers crossed behind backs.

❣

That year, I had a crush of my own.

His name was Peter Crayford, and I had never felt like this before. Of course, I'd thought that about every person I'd had a crush on previously, but *this* one was different.

The crush hit me without warning, as most crushes seem to do. I was standing outside Miss Prentice's English class, waiting for the bell to ring, when I overheard a conversation between Peter and Louisa Rose. We'd just come from a school assembly, where Louisa had made an announcement about collecting canned food to donate to the Salvation Army for Christmas.

'Collecting food, are you?' he asked her.

'Yes,' Louisa replied. She was a brainy type, very straightforward and clever in that way that can also make people come across as a bit weird sometimes.

'I'll bring you some canned asparagus,' he said.

To be clear, this was not a funny exchange. But there was something very droll about the way he said it, enunciating every syllable of *as-par-a-gus* (which is also, obviously, the least appealing of the canned food family). For a girl raised on the scathing wit of Rowan Atkinson and his legendary turn as Edmund Blackadder, it had the effect of lighting a bonfire in my heart.

I snorted and tried to cover my laughter, but I needn't have worried. I wasn't on Peter Crayford's radar, and he wouldn't have noticed how the world had suddenly tilted on its axis.

Because I was so new to the school, I hadn't known who Peter was before that morning and I immediately made it my mission to find out as much about him as I could. He wasn't the kind of person you immediately noticed when you walked into a room, existing somewhere outside of the genre of teen heart-throbs that have graced every school in existence and will forevermore. His eyes were a little close together and he had what could be derisively described as 'girlish hips', but for whatever reason he still floated on the periphery of the in-crowd (where conventionally unattractive boys are often able to find a home, unlike their female counterparts). But these flaws only made him more appealing to me. He was funny (*clearly*) but he was also physically flawed. It didn't seem preposterous to fantasise about a series of firsts with him, because in many ways we were surely the same.

We were both awkward-looking and slightly portly, a kinship I felt he would appreciate, this being before I understood how audaciously unaware men can be of their own physical appearance when it comes to choosing a mate. I learned he was a year older than the others in our class, and I felt I was too—*intellectually speaking*. He was a swimmer, and apparently a very good one. I have a very vivid memory of him walking along the side of a pool, poured into a pair of Speedos, goggles wrapped tightly around his face. He stops to look up at the stands and, staring straight at me, pushes his goggles up to his forehead and smiles, brown eyes crinkling at the corners. I can recall it so clearly, this scene, and decades later it still has the power to halt me in my tracks.

But of course, it's not a memory at all. It's something I brought into being in the confines of my own head, a bit of glamour given form by the powerful magic of a teenage girl's deepest desires. Still, I see it there as if it really happened. And when we're dealing with memory, who's to say what's real and what's not?

English was the only class that Peter and I shared, which seemed a stroke of good luck to me. It was my best subject, which made it my favourite class, and I took full advantage of the opportunity to show off how smart I was. At fifteen I still laboured under the delusion that boys would be impressed by clever girls—a terrible miscalculation, I think you'll agree.

I learned about Peter's music preferences during one such class, when Miss Prentice directed us to give an oral presentation on a song of our choice. Chelsea Brown (our year's resident Mean Girl, with a pinched mouth and a vicious tongue) delivered a very earnest and passionate speech on Everclear's 'Heroin Girl', the basic upshot being that drugs are bad and none of us should ever take them.

Mine was a less cerebral contribution, a comedic assassination of Gina G's chart-topping club hit, 'Ooh Aah . . . Just a Little Bit'. Miss Prentice loved it, which in turn infuriated Chelsea, who stayed behind after class to argue against my good grade because 'she didn't even talk about the music, she just bagged the song!'—which is actually a fair point, but humour always wins over a crowd. I don't make the rules, baby.

But the person whose presentation I really looked forward to seeing that day was Peter's, and he didn't disappoint. Although I maintained a laser-like focus on his activities throughout each of our English classes, I'd barely heard him say more than a few sentences. Most of his time was spent leaning backwards in his chair and slowly rocking back and forth, the universal dialect of bored adolescent boys. This would be the first time I'd heard him properly *speak*, and I was excited.

When Miss Prentice called on him, I assumed the calm veneer of someone trying not to arouse suspicion, but my insides were churning. For the next five minutes, I would be given unencumbered permission to stare directly at the object of my fancy. To gaze at his face, his lips, his eyes. To take in his unusually long and slender fingers, clutched as they were around the piece of lined, A4 paper on which I could see his scrawled handwriting. I knew I wouldn't have another opportunity like this for a while—certainly not before the end of term and the long, endless, unfilled days of summer that awaited us all. I needed to make the next five minutes count.

I can tell you with total sincerity that I have never been more interested in hearing about The Beatles than I was in Miss Prentice's classroom that day, nor have I ever learned as little about a subject while staring intently at the person delivering a thesis on it. I did learn, however, that they were Peter Crayford's favourite band and that his hair was silkier in the front than I'd thought, despite the constant immersion in chlorine. I learned that his lips were formed in a perfect Cupid's bow, and his front two teeth were slightly crooked (a feature common to most of the people I've loved, I've realised).

I had never really cared for The Beatles. (I still don't. I would feel embarrassed about dismissing *The Greatest Band of All Time* as 'overrated', but men have been doing that to women's art for centuries, so I don't really care. Also, teenage girls discovered and popularised The Beatles, but they only became enshrined as rock'n'roll legends when men decided they were good, so, again, I don't really care.) But the knowledge that *Peter* loved The Beatles was all the incentive I needed to become an instant superfan. (*'Yeah . . . I'm pretty into J-J-J'.*)

Prior to this, the only music I had ever bought was the mainstream jazz CDs I found in discount bins at the local Sanity. I had numerous 'best of' CDs featuring Ella Fitzgerald, Billie Holiday and Dinah Washington, my reasoning at the time being that the *purchasing* of music itself was somehow the same thing as having a personality, and so it didn't matter that my collection consisted of multiple versions of essentially the same playlists, give or take a song here or there. After class that day, I swapped out the jazz and started stockpiling 'best of' collections of The Beatles, and I'd sit in my room and play the songs over and over, pretending to myself that I liked them, because it made me feel closer to Peter.

That was the summer John Lennon's posthumously released single 'Free as a Bird' hit the airwaves, and it played on high rotation in the local Wendy's, where I worked as a professional hot dog eater and occasional ice-cream scooper. Every time the song's opening bars came over the loudspeaker, I took it as a cosmic sign. *It's our song!* I'd think to myself, my cheeks growing almost as pink as the shorts that formed part of the Wendy's uniform code—which, given their luminosity, was no mean feat I can tell you. I imagined us dancing to it at a social gathering, both of us swaying slowly in time with the music, my head resting comfortably on his shoulder (a detail that might have proved difficult in real life, given we were the same height), his hand resting gently on the small of my back.

Clementine, he would whisper.

Yes? I'd murmur back.

I like you, he'd say. *Like*, like-*like you.*

I like you too, I'd reply. *Like*, like-*like you.*

And then he would kiss me, and it would be wonderful and perfect and exactly how I'd imagined. A circle of people would form around us and cheer loudly, some of them giving him congratulatory slaps on the back while I stood there, his arm draped loosely over my shoulders, looking embarrassed but also incredibly thrilled to have finally been picked.

Oh, that poor, sweet, darling girl! How much I feel for her!

For whom among us has not fantasised in this way about someone whose love we so optimistically yearn for? Have we not all longed to be desired not just by these objects of affection, but recognised as *worthy* of them by our peers? To be thought of as a suitable match? To walk into a room, transformed and glorious, met by the wide eyes and whispered shock of those people who would be surprised not just to discover we have an interior life of dreams and wishes ourselves, but that we exist at all?

❣

I had learned early on that I wasn't considered an appropriate candidate for Trinity's Cool Group after Jenny Turner invited and then uninvited me to a party at Nathan Crabb's house. The invitation had been issued in science class, a few days after our first conversation.

'Hey,' she said, turning around in her chair. 'What are you doing on Friday night?'

'Um . . .' I replied, making a pretence of mentally running through my calendar as if it were filled to the brim with social engagements. 'I don't think I have anything on that night.'

'Great!' she said. 'Nathan's having a party! You should come.'

'Really?!' I exclaimed (again, too eagerly). 'I mean . . . if you're sure that would be okay?'

'Yeah!' Jenny said. 'I mean, I have to check with him first, but I'm sure it will be fine. Why wouldn't it be?'

Let me dispel any fears you might have that this was a set-up. It wasn't. Jenny was and still is one of the nicest people I know—a rare example of someone who happens to be super popular and also just a genuinely very excellent human. But the social strata of high school is a complex beast. We all have our place in it, and it can be difficult to swim against the current even when you're a big fish.

For a few days, the party lived in my head as a beacon.
I started planning an outfit and thinking about the logistics.
Would there be alcohol? Should I bring my own? Who would
I talk to? How could I be as cool as possible? Would I meet
Jenny and her friends there, or beforehand? I knew Nathan
lived near me, which meant I could walk and save myself
the humiliation of having my dad deliver me. On the other
hand, would I feel better being ferried there in a car, buoyed
by his unwavering love right up until the crucial moment of
being dropped into the shark cage? There were so many hard
decisions to make.

'I've been invited to a party this weekend,' I mentioned casually to my parents one night over dinner.

'Oh?' they murmured in response, glancing at each other.
'Whose party?'

'Nathan Crabb's,' I replied. And then, because the names of
my peers meant very little to them, I followed up with, 'He's a
boy at school.'

'Right,' my mother said. 'And will his parents be home?'

'I expect so,' I said. 'But even if they're not, it's just down
the road.'

'And how do you know Nathan?' my father asked, looking
up from his pasta.

'I told you,' I said. 'He's a boy at *school*?'

They looked at each other.

'Well?' I prompted, beginning to get agitated.

'Well, what?' my mother replied.

'Well, can I *go*?'

She shrugged. 'Sure, I don't see why not.'

Inside, I beamed. It seemed impossible to believe my good fortune. I was going to a *party*! With the cool kids! And I'd only just started at the new school!

I shouldn't have got my hopes up. The next day, Jenny turned to me in science and said, 'I'm so sorry, but you're not going to be able to come to the party.'

'Oh!' I replied, crestfallen.

'I'm really sorry,' she repeated. 'It's just that Nathan's only allowed to have a certain number of people. When I asked him if you could come, he said it was just impossible.'

'No, it's fine,' I said, trying to remove all trace of feeling from my voice. 'I understand, of course.'

'Honestly, it's just a weird thing about numbers,' she said. 'It's not you.' She paused. 'I really wanted you to come.'

'I get it,' I said, smiling at her.

She smiled back. 'I'll make sure you're invited to the next one,' she said.

'Sure!' I said, trying to sound upbeat. 'That'd be fun!'

She turned back to her work, but after a few seconds she turned back to me.

'It really is just about the numbers,' she said.

'I know,' I told her. 'It makes total sense.'

That night, I told my parents I'd decided not to go to the party after all, and when Friday rolled around I went to bed early.

I lay there with the window open, listening to the sounds of the weekend unfolding outside. I imagined that every noise I heard, every bang, every moment of potential revelry, was coming from Nathan Crabb's house. So many people, having so much fun.

But the numbers. Of course we had to worry about the numbers. It made sense.

❣

It wasn't as if I were completely friendless. I'd met a girl early on who was just like me—nerdy, not conventionally beautiful and yet to come into her true power. But Natalie was more at ease with herself than I was, possibly because she had already found the man she had pledged the rest of her life to. His name was Jesus Christ, and they had a pretty strong relationship, despite his having been dead for almost 2000 years.

I had dipped my toe into religion a handful of times and found that it wasn't for me, but I admired Natalie's devotion. She was different to the weird evangelicals who lived next door to us, whose church youth group I had once attended in a desperate attempt to make friends, but then never returned to for fear I might be accidentally drowned during a forced baptism-gone-wrong. Natalie was funny and kind and—I was pretty sure—would never try to kill me.

Our friendship began in the schoolyard one day when we discovered a mutual love of the television sketch comedy show *Full Frontal*. One of our favourite things to do was mimic the comedic stylings of a young Eric Bana, whose impression of

A Current Affair's Ray Martin had us in stitches. We christened ourselves after two of the recurring characters, nudists named Beulah and Neville who loved to do everything 'in the nude'. Natalie was Beulah and I was Neville and we cracked ourselves up laughing at the rude absurdity of it all.

In between our impersonations and improv, we talked about boys. I told Natalie about Peter and swore her to secrecy, and she offered up a crush of her own to seal the contract. She was hopelessly in love with Christopher Sanderson, an academically brilliant wunderkind who was smart and funny and cute and, as he would tell me a few years later, terribly burdened at the time by his hidden homosexuality.

Natalie's family was moving to Whyalla in the summer, and I was devastated. She was definitely 'my people', and I had so few of them. Still, we made the most of the time we had and determined to enjoy ourselves. We formed what we called Crush Club, which really just involved the two of us talking in code about Peter and Christopher and occasionally passing notes to each other that extolled their respective virtues. We claimed to be terrified the letters would be intercepted and our secrets discovered, yet there was a tiny part of both of us that relished the thought of what such an occurrence might provoke. The planting of a seed. The catalyst that might force *something* to happen, finally.

Life, beginning.

❣

With the long and decidedly Peter-free summer looming before me, I was thrilled to hear that Jenny and her friends had petitioned the school to allow the year tens to have an end-of-term social with the school agreeing on the proviso they do all the work to promote it. Having organised events now as an adult, this memory makes me laugh. What additional 'promotion' could possibly be involved for an event held exclusively for the members of an institution they're forced to attend every day and thus cannot help but hear about repeatedly? Still, I suppose it was meant to function as a lesson in responsibility, and few people rise to a planning challenge better than teenage girls.

Signs began appearing around the school with YEAR TEN SOCIAL!!!!! blaring out from them in bubble writing. The dance would be held on the last Friday of term, which meant it would also be the last day either of us were able to see our crushes: Natalie for eternity and me for six weeks, which felt like practically the same thing. We were *beside* ourselves, and we weren't the only ones. Practically the whole grade was fizzy about it, with no teacher spared from the endless chatter about who was going with whom and who was planning to wear what.

To this last point, Crush Club paid considerable attention. We pondered different outfits for hours, listing the pros and cons of each with the seriousness of a militia going off to war. Fashion was not my strong suit, what with all the caftans and chinos, but I felt like I could pull together *something* that might create a wow factor. I'd scoured all the op shops in town for what I thought were their best goods, and I indulged in hours of daydreams in which I walked slowly into the disco room to the sound of appreciative whispers and wide-eyed awe. *Wow, I heard them saying. She looks amazing.*

I hadn't had much experience of being considered desirable by the opposite sex, which is to say I hadn't had any, but I'd watched a significant number of movies in which awkward ugly ducklings were transformed into swans. I wanted that for myself, and I really believed it might be possible. I wanted to know what it felt like to walk into a room and feel like Laney Boggs in *She's All That*, or Louise Miller in *Teen Witch*. I had lived in a fantasy world inside my head for so long, casting myself in the role of the brilliant, brave and beautiful heroine; the girl who everybody *wants* to get the guy because it makes total sense for him to get her too. I saw myself playing her so clearly. Was it so crazy to want other people to see me playing her too? Was it so out of left field to imagine Peter could see me as someone like her, captivating and magnetic, someone he would be proud to be seen with in front of the fastidiously judgemental people he called friends?

Once again, I want to reach back through the years and hold the girl I used to be. Maybe she was all of us, lost and alone and insecure. Trying on different outfits and styles to see what she could fit into rather than looking for the things that could fit her.

We were all so beautiful then, and we had no idea.

❣

Time has an irritating habit of moving both quickly and slowly at the same time, and so it was that the end-of-year dance seemed to take years to arrive and yet was upon us before we knew it. By mid-morning, our teachers had given up on trying to contain us. It was the last day of school and summer had truly arrived, so they let us have our intrigues and gossip as a parting gift.

I raced home that afternoon, my insides churning. I only had a few hours to get ready, and not a moment to waste. Endless planning with Natalie had seen me arrive at what I felt was the perfect outfit. I'd chosen a short slip dress in black (slimming) and sheer black tights (an unusual choice for the summer, but something I'd seen women wear to great effect in the romantic comedies I consumed voraciously) with a battered old pair of Doc Marten boots that I believed would give me the same kind of edge Jenny Turner had approved of all those weeks ago. I added a brown polyester jacket I'd found in the men's section at a local op shop. It was hot and sweaty, but it was a nod to the androgyny that had brought me so much sartorial comfort in this and previous years. I completed the look by tying a floral silk scarf around my neck—a touch of elegance befitting a dance.

As I knotted the scarf, I stood before the rickety wardrobe and looked in the crooked mirror. On the whole, I was pleased. I had tried my best with what I had, and the rest was out of my control. I tugged at the bottom of the jacket, twisting from side to side to see how well it covered the heft of my bottom, then turned back to face the mirror full on.

'This is it,' I said to my reflection. 'This is the night we've been waiting for.'

I leaned towards the mirror and applied some of my mother's lipstick, a discarded tube of Chanel in a dark mulberry colour. I pressed my lips together, put the tube in my shoulder bag and went to the lounge room, where my father was waiting to drive me back to school.

❣

I have a photograph from this night of me standing on the gravel driveway that led to the back of my parents' house (the space between 'upstairs' and 'downstairs'—our version of a mezzanine). The sun is beginning to set and the sky behind me is streaked with orange. I'm looking at the camera and smiling the tremulous smile of fifteen-year-old girls everywhere.

There is so much to love about this girl and the wonderful, terrible optimism shining in her eyes.

She is about to have her heart broken.

❣

I walked from the drop-off car park to the north of the school and tentatively entered the small assembly hall. There were flashing lights placed intermittently around the room, but I tried to avoid those. Years before, in another school and another country, an old science teacher had once told me that looking straight at burning magnesium for too long would sear your retinas and render you instantly blind. Admittedly, this was an unlikely risk with $12.95 fairy lights from Bunnings, but I had made it a rule to be careful around any light source of dubious origin. As a chronic hypochondriac, I assumed I would lose my sight one day—I just didn't want it to be before Peter Crayford and I had shared in the transformative experience of our first water birth.

Natalie and I quickly found each other and, alcohol having not yet entered our lives as a social lubricant, made an awkward show of dancing together while furtively scanning the room. By this stage, I had developed a finely tuned radar for Peter's whereabouts and all conceivable movements, and I spotted him almost immediately.

Play it cool, I thought to myself, my arms swinging by my sides as I shuffled to the unforgiving beat of Smashing Pumpkins' 'Today'.

He was standing in the 'cool' corner of the room, that unmarked space that seems to become protected by an invisible force field the moment someone of high social rank steps into it. His hair was doing that adorable floppy thing I liked so much, and he was wearing a red-and-black acrylic jumper that hung just below his hips. He was leaning against the wall, and I could see him smiling as he chatted with someone.

Natalie was telling me a joke and I was trying to make it seem like I was paying attention, but every fibre of my being was trained on Peter. It's a terrible habit that has followed me into adulthood, this inability to follow a conversation if someone in my proximity has captured my attention. It plagues me with crushes and exes alike, a hyper instinct for where they are and, more importantly, who they're talking to. I have cried so many tears late at night after men I loved have gone home with women with whom I knew, *just knew*, something was brewing, maybe even before they knew it themselves.

Natalie delivered the punchline to her joke and I made a huge show of laughing, reasoning that being seen by Peter in the act of being diverted by something hilarious would endear me to him—again, an unsupported thesis that follows us all into adulthood. I finished heaving my shoulders and suggested we go outside. It was stuffy inside the hall, and my jacket was made of non-breathable fibres.

Outside, Natalie and I found a quiet corner and set to forensically dissecting the situation. It was true neither of the boys had looked in our direction, but as far as we could tell they weren't looking at any other girls either. (In Christopher Sanderson's case, this would turn out to be an early clue.) We recounted everything we'd observed about their body language, which led to us talking about their bodies and repeating, for what must have been the millionth time, exactly what it was we found 'soooooooooooo cute!' about them.

Sometime in the middle of our conversation, a shadow fell across us. I looked up to see the figure of Gavin Murdoch standing there.

'What are youse girls talking about?' he asked.

Gavin was a perfect example of the inherent inequity of high school's cool politics, being one of the many boys allowed entry to the inner sanctum despite being physically repulsive, absolutely bereft of personality and as interesting as a bag of bricks. Popular girls can be many things—boring, cruel, vapid—but never are they allowed to be anything less than physically angelic. I would estimate eighty percent of the popular boys at my high school were grotesque (with that percentage actually increasing alongside their popularity), but for some reason they had managed to convince themselves otherwise. I apologise to the twenty-five-year-old women many of them are aiming to date now—if we had understood the unbearable levels of audacity we were condoning back then, perhaps we would have staged an intervention.

Natalie and I looked up at Gavin.

'Oh, you know,' I said. 'We're just talking about . . . stuff.'

He took a seat next to us. 'Talking about anyone in particular?'

'No,' Natalie said. She was a lot smarter than me, and she'd dealt with these people for a lot longer.

'C'mon,' he said, 'youse must've been talking about *someone* to be outside. Tell me!'

To this day, I have no idea what compelled me. Perhaps it was his affable manner, which made it seem as if he liked us and was on our side. Maybe—and this is probably the truth of the matter—it was because I wanted something to happen. Good or bad, I wanted to blow the whole situation up so that *something* would occur and I could move on from whatever purgatory I seemed to be stuck in, plagued by the same daydreams and tormented by the same lack of progress. Whatever the reason, I spilled the beans.

'Well,' I said to him, 'I do have a crush on someone.'

'G'orn, tell me!' he exclaimed, leaning towards me.

'No!' I screeched. 'As if I would tell you! You'll just go and tell everyone!'

'Nah, I won't,' he said. 'Promise. G'orn, just tell me!'

I took a deep breath and looked at Natalie. Her eyes were giving me mixed messages, with *this-is-a-bad-idea-and-on-your-own-head-be-it* on the one hand, and *ooh-do-it-this-could-be-great!* on the other

I took a deep breath. 'Okay.'

I told Gavin the whole story and made him promise— *promise!*—not to leak a word of it to anyone.

He swore that he would never so much as even think about it again, stood up and gave me a friendly pat on the shoulder.

'See youse!' he said, and left us both on the bench.

Natalie and I gossiped for a few minutes longer and then decided to re-enter the building. We moved past groups of students talking and laughing, some of them holding hands. I felt unburdened in some way. I had confessed a secret and I hadn't been laughed at. Perhaps it wasn't so ridiculous after all, to imagine myself paired with this boy who could freely pass through that force field without any problems? Maybe I could do that too?

I stepped into the hall and realised how very, very wrong I was.

❣

You know that moment in a high school movie when the protagonist realises that everything is set against her and the entire social system she's been wading through is preparing to flush her down the proverbial toilet? Less Andie Walsh in *Pretty in Pink*, and more Josie Grossie in *Never Been Kissed*?

That's what it was like.

As I walked back into the room that night, nothing was visibly different. But there had been a distinct shift in energy. You know how in that same movie, we'd be shown cutaways to different whispered reactions? That's what it was like too, except I could sense and see them all in my head at the same time. I knew—I just *knew*—that something had changed. A secret had entered the space and been received with wild enthusiasm, and what I was sensing was the sudden realisation that the owner of that secret—me—had just walked into the room.

I told Natalie I needed to get something from my bag and walked to the side of the hall where I had casually thrown it on the ground. I made a show of rummaging around in it, cheeks burning, and when I looked up *Gavin fucking Murdoch* was standing there.

'Hey,' he said.

'You!' I exclaimed. 'I can't fucking believe you! I told you not to say anything, but obviously you have!'

He held his hands up as if in surrender. 'What are you talking about?! I didn't say a thing, I promise!'

'Really?' I spat. 'Because it feels a lot like you fucking did!'

'Nah!' he said. 'I swear!'

I took a deep breath. But just as I opened my mouth to speak again, Peter Crayford walked up. I stared at him as he leaned against the wall, looking at me.

'Hey,' he said, after an uncomfortably long silence. 'Can I talk to you outside for a bit?'

I looked at him. This was the closest I'd ever been to him in my life. It was the first time he'd ever spoken to me. And he was standing there, asking me if I'd like to talk with him. Outside. *For a bit.*

From behind him, I could see Gavin give me an enthusiastic thumbs-up.

'Sure!' I said, trying to sound light. 'That'd be great.'

As I went to follow Peter out, Gavin grabbed my arm. 'Good one!' he said.

I smiled and took a deep breath.

'Wish me luck!' I said, still thinking that he'd done me some kind of favour. I was Allison Reynolds at the end of *The Breakfast Club*, Nicole Maris in the final scene of *Drive Me Crazy*, Drew Barrymore in anything. It seemed possible that every moment of every daydream I'd had about Peter Crayford specifically was about to be realised, and all I'd had to do was believe. *Thank you, Gavin Murdoch!* I thought to myself as I walked towards the door. *You've done me a huge favour!*

To use the common parlance of the internet . . . LOL.

❣

Peter was standing by one of the benches when I found him outside. He had one foot up on the wooden slats of the bench, his body bent over the crooked leg so I couldn't see his face properly.

'Hi!' I said, when I got there.

He didn't say anything in response, so I continued.

'Um . . . okay. So, you've probably heard people inside saying that I like you.'

Still nothing.

'And . . . it's true.'

Oh yeah, keeping it real smooth.

Throughout my declaration, Peter kept his head down, nodding occasionally. I waited, wondering what he was thinking. Would we talk first and then kiss, or kiss and then talk? I decided I would let him lead the way. But just as I was preparing to lean forward and close my eyes, he stood up, spun his body away from me and walked back inside.

He hadn't said a word. He hadn't even looked at me, not once during the whole exchange.

Almost twenty-five years have passed since that night, and I've endured countless more romantic indignities with many of them more objectively terrible. But the heart of a fifteen-year-old girl is precious. It hasn't yet grown familiar with the sensation of being bruised and broken, nor does it know what it feels like to be healed and made stronger, the calcified scars protecting its soft and gentle insides. The heart of a fifteen-year-old girl believes that the love she holds is a powerful magic, and she stands ready and willing to give it away as an act of faith alone.

How many of us have watched as that gift is thrown back at our feet, crumpled and streaked with mud, and come to the conclusion not that the recipient of our love was unworthy, but that the love itself—*our* love—was just not good enough?

I stood there, my heart's love bruised and whimpering on the floor, and I felt scorn for it. This stupid love, this pathetic love, this embarrassing, *sad* love and its great galumph of a girl. What a fine joke we were! How we had made everyone laugh!

I kicked the love and watched it weep and then, not wanting to leave it on the ground for anyone else to find—because as bad a love as it was, it was still *my* love—I picked it up and held it. I sat on the bench with the love in my lap and together we looked at the night sky. I would not cry. Not here. I wouldn't give them that. In my lap, I felt the love steel itself and listened as its tears and weeping subsided too.

Eventually, I returned to the hall. The night was drawing to a close and soon people would be making their way to the car park to be picked up by parents or, in the case of girls like Jenny Turner, older boyfriends.

I could sense heads turning my way, but I ignored them all and held mine higher. They could laugh at me all they liked, but I wouldn't give them the satisfaction of thinking they had beaten me. It was a definitive moment; I had lost something that night, but I had found something too: a strength and resolve I hadn't known existed inside me but whose flame was beginning to flicker and burn. Long after I'd forgotten the names and faces of the people in the hall that night, the flame would still be with me, a raging bonfire to light my way through the darkest of nights.

I pushed my way through the crowd and found Natalie. She didn't ask me what had happened but instead pulled me into a hug and said, 'Oh my God, Neville, I'm going to miss you so much!'

'I'm going to miss you too, Beulah. Promise you'll write to me!'

'I promise,' she replied. 'Let's dance!'

We joined a circle of other girls and shook our bodies together, singing along and laughing. I was still dying inside, but it felt better to be dying with these girls than to be dying alone.

Somewhere during the third chorus of a Backstreet Boys song, Natalie grabbed me and whispered into my ear, 'I'll be right back.'

I watched as she walked to the makeshift stage and approached the DJ. They chatted for a few moments, and then he passed her the microphone. The music cut out, and she stood in front of everyone. She was leaving in a few days and she had nothing to lose.

'I just wanted to say that I'm really going to miss you all!' She stood there, beaming her bright, beautiful smile at everyone, a lot of whom didn't deserve to be included in that statement. 'I've loved knowing all of you, and I hope you guys have a great next couple of years!'

She paused.

'I also want to say this. Christopher Sanderson, I love you! Will you dance with me?'

The room erupted in cheers and whoops as the opening bars of Whitney Houston's 'I Will Always Love You' started to play.

Natalie handed the microphone back to the DJ, stepped off the stage and walked up to where Christopher stood. She smiled at him, the smile of a person who means no harm and is asking for nothing except the pleasure of a dance. The *last* dance.

He took her hand and gave it to her, this simple gift. And as people started to dance around them, some in groups and some in couples, they swayed together and didn't stop until the final bars had faded to nothing and the lights had come back on.

❣

I kept it together that night, through the humiliating goodbyes and the see-you-next-years, through the long drive home with my father, who wanted to know how the night went. I could bear the heartache for myself, but I knew I couldn't stand seeing him watch me cry. And so I kept it in and told him I'd had a great time, and blinked back the tears that had threatened to spill over the moment I got into the car. I plastered a smile on my face for my mother, who had made me a cup of tea, and when I'd finished that I yawned loudly, claiming tiredness and an early morning wake-up to work at the ice-cream shop.

It wasn't until I was safely in bed that I let myself feel the crushing humiliation and disappointment of it all, and the tears flowed out of me in a deluge. I replayed the scene over and over in my mind, the agony of it piercing me anew. It was more than just the rejection that hurt—it was what the rejection confirmed about me. That I would never be good enough, never suitable enough, never interesting enough or funny enough or, most importantly of all, beautiful enough. It was so unfair to me that other girls seemed to have it so easy. Of course, I know now that all girls suffer in one way or another, some more than others, but this wouldn't have even occurred to me back when I was comparing myself to the ones with slim calves, small waists and what seemed like an endless parade of boyfriends or perhaps even just one or two very steady ones.

Eventually I fell into a fitful sleep, exhausted and spent. When I woke, I remembered I wouldn't have to see Peter Crayford at school the following week, and the thought both consoled and tormented me in equal measure.

❣

I survived, as we all surprise ourselves by doing. I spent most of the summer working at the ice-cream store. I stopped listening to The Beatles (a silver lining) and resumed the purchasing of Ella Fitzgerald CDs and oversized caftans. Natalie and I wrote letters and spoke on the phone for a while, until we didn't, which is how these things go. We reconnected on Facebook a few years ago. She has a son now, like me, and has learned a lot about the world through her dealings with men, also like me. She's one of the strongest people I know. I consider it one of my life's great privileges to be in her orbit, and to be known by her.

I thought of Peter frequently during the long school break, circling his home address in the White Pages and dotting it with hearts. It gave me comfort to look at it, imagining him at home on his bed, his chair, at his family's dinner table. I have a memory, buried somewhere in the reams of stories and mental detritus I've acquired since then, of sending him a letter. I was certain I had misunderstood him somehow or been misunderstood by him, and I sought to clarify the situation. Whether or not he ever received it I don't know, but it was never mentioned. I returned to school at the start of the new year, anxious and excited, terrified to see him yet also craving the fix I had been without for so long. I saw him standing in the courtyard on that first day, near Miss Prentice's class and the site where my infatuation first began. He was walking with someone, or perhaps he was on his own. The truth is, I can't remember. Because although I tried to summon the strength of feeling that had plagued me for so many months, I found that it had been replaced by just the barest flutter, and this too disappeared within a matter of days. He was just a boy after all, neither god nor monster.

He tried to kiss me once, when school had finished and we were all celebrating our graduation at a friend's house on the river. I had found my place in the social hierarchy by this stage, figuring out at last how to pass through that invisible force field that had captivated me for so long. I moved between the two worlds, knowing I belonged to neither of them fully, but being okay with it nonetheless.

We were standing on the banks of the river at night, having what might have been the first and last real conversation we would ever have. Suddenly, he lurched towards me, and I instinctively pulled back.

'What are you doing?' I asked, vaguely incredulous. 'Don't you remember the year ten social?'

He looked at me blankly.

'I told you I liked you and you brutally ignored me!'

He laughed. 'Come on, Clem, that was so long ago!'

And he's right. It was so long ago.

It was so long ago, and it was yesterday, and we are forty years old now but we will be fifteen forever.

Like so many things, it turns out the story of loving a boy is really the story of loving a girl.

Me.

SWEETIE

When I was twelve, my family moved from the desert heat of Oman to the freezing, windswept coast of Norfolk in the UK and, having become friendless overnight, I found myself with a sudden surplus of time. The prospect of having to make new friends made me anxious, so I did the next best thing: I got a job.

Every Sunday, I'd wake at the cruel hour of 5.30 am and, yawning, walk to the local newsagent. This was almost thirty years ago, when young girls in small towns weren't discouraged from wandering the streets in the dark to deliver newspapers. It seems astonishing now but, then, so do a lot of things about the nineties, not least of which was the widely accepted sexual appeal of Ethan Hawke.

It took around two hours to deliver all the newspapers, but I sometimes stretched it out to three if there was anything good in the tabloids that day. There was a bench on the top of a hill towards the end of my route, and I liked to sit there as the sun came up and read about the wide array of Tory politicians who'd been caught on tape engaged in what was always referred to gleefully as 'lewd sex acts'.

I'd come home with black ink smeared across my fingers, the little paper bag with my wages already empty and thrown away. I was paid the princely sum of two pounds, which I mostly spent on lollies at the corner store. Within two years, I'd graduate to buying cigarettes and turns on the slot machines in the town's penny arcade, but for now I am living a simpler, more age appropriate life.

At home, my mother would still be asleep. She wasn't what you'd call an early riser.

❣

The paper round didn't last long, mainly because I kept getting in trouble for reading them before the people who'd ordered them could. This was in the midst of Charles and Diana's separation, and I was spending a lot of time on the bench reading the various takes. The final straw came at the end of one particularly scandal-filled week, when a customer complained I had taken four hours to arrive. Her morning had been ruined, she said, which seemed to me somewhat hyperbolic considering the woes of the Princess. My boss didn't agree, and thus my short-lived stint as a newsie came to an end. School was going wonderfully well too, as I'm sure you can imagine given I was still coated in a thick layer of puppy fat, covered in freckles and, due to years spent living in a desert, ignorant in matters of great cultural import. To give you some idea, I thought the lead singer of Nirvana was called Kirk O'Bain, and I would confidently refer to him as such whenever his genius was discussed, which was frequently.

I did have some sense of the social hierarchy, though, and I knew where all the most popular girls in my year worked: they were ice-cream scoopers at the Sweet Shack, down near the jetty. On hot days, the line for the Mr Whippy cones would stretch all the way down to the seaside. I had started working at a bakery across the street, which was significantly less glamorous and rather more yeast-filled. As I packaged bread and fairy buns for harried mothers, I would stare at the Sweeties, whose long hair was always being loosened and then pulled back into new ponytails, their jewellery jangling as they leaned out the serving window to hand someone three double soft serves with a Flake.

I'm going to work there one day, I said to myself. I was turning thirteen soon, and was officially giving myself permission to 'dream big'.

❣

The Sweet Shack was owned by a man named Roger, whose weathered skin and nicotine-stained beard made him look every single one of his thirty-five years, plus about twenty more on top of that. I could see him as he leaned against the doorframe between the shop and its back room, chain-smoking cigarettes and yelling at the football on the television.

He's so cool, I thought.

I had asked him for a job before, popping into the shop one afternoon on my way home from school. It was April, and the town was just starting to thaw after the long, cold winter. There was still a sharp breeze rolling in from the North Sea, but the salt in it was noticeably thicker and more fertile now—a sure sign that summer was on its way. One of the Sweeties was working the window as I walked in, a girl named Donna who was in my year at school. Despite the chill in the air, she was optimistically bare-shouldered, black bra straps and the lacy trim of the cups visible beneath a skimpy blue singlet.

She nodded to me. 'Hey.'

'Hi!' I piped back, too enthusiastically.

Roger looked up from his position in the doorframe and briefly removed the cigarette clamped between his lips. 'What c'n I get you?' he drawled.

'Actually,' I said, 'I was wondering if you're looking for any more staff?'

To my right, I could hear Donna taking someone's order at the window.

'Got any experience?' he asked, looking me up and down.

'Not with ice cream,' I replied. 'But I've been working in the bakery across the road for a bit, and I'm a fast learner!'

He put the cigarette to his mouth and took a long drag.

'Well'—he had already turned his attention back to the screen and its seemingly endless broadcast of football matches—'we're all full up at the moment. But keep checking in, something might come up.'

'Thanks,' I said, standing there for another beat before turning to the entrance. 'Well . . . see ya,' I called out over my shoulder.

The sound of sudden cheering blared out from the television as Roger simultaneously swore. Donna, leaning against the counter inspecting her nails, looked up.

'Bye,' she replied, staring indifferently at me.

❣

I lost my job at the bakery not long after this ('You're too distracted—stop staring out the window all day long!') but was gratified to discover that an abundance of short-term employment opportunities arise when a sleepy seaside town enters its summer season. The Sweet Shack's roster remained full, but I was hired instead by a competing ice-cream parlour not far down the street. It was much smaller (in fact, I was the only employee aside from the elderly couple who owned it) and far less cool, but I reasoned it would give me the experience I needed to convince Roger of my dairy-wielding capabilities.

The husband of the pair was old and cranky, but he was nice enough in his own way. He allowed me incremental access to responsibility, at first only allowing me to serve candy to the parade of tourists and locals who sought to satisfy their sweet tooth on the way to or from the pebble-lined beach. After days of proving I could handle doling out chocolate freckles in small paper bags, he let me start taking the payments for them, teaching me how to enter the numbers into the till like I was a child learning the names of animals for the first time. Finally, having mastered both the art of counting out sweets and then counting out the change, he taught me how to pull a Mr Whippy.

The trick to a soft serve is to remain calm. Don't be overwhelmed by how fast the ice cream comes out of the tap; hold your cone hand steady and rotate your wrist, starting wide and then layering it up to a single point. Pull enough of them and it becomes second nature. The hardest were the double cones, but even they became easy once you learned how to adjust the tiny muscles in your hand and brace against the change in weight.

For someone who had chosen a line of work that required face-to-face contact with the public, the old man didn't like people much, and soon enough I replaced him in the window. I was paid two pounds an hour, and my shifts usually lasted around three hours. As grateful as I was to have the job, I felt the disparity in glamour between me and the Sweeties keenly. Unlike those golden girls with their exposed bras and short skirts, I had a strict uniform—a white polo shirt with black trousers, and a blue apron to wear over the top. Despite my best intentions, I still hadn't managed to lose any weight—weight that I hadn't really noticed when I was younger but that was becoming more of a problem the further I moved away from childhood. I wanted so badly to be thin, and yet couldn't resist the allure of the hot chips doused in salt and vinegar that you could buy from the fish shop down the road. Later, at home, I'd gaze at myself in the mirror and feel nothing but disgust for this fat and loathsome creature who would never attain the shine of the Sweeties, who all seemed to know exactly how to *be* in the world.

I was glad not to be working across the street from them anymore. The distance meant I was able to slink in and out of work without being seen, and I was silently grateful for the opportunity to exist for a while longer out of their sight. I was afflicted by the contradiction of both self-loathing and narcissism that befalls so many thirteen-year-olds, convinced I was the singular focus of everyone I knew or had ever met, all of whom pitied me at best or were outright disgusted by me at worst.

I began to steer clear of the Sweet Shack when I walked home at the end of each shift, embarrassed by my daggy uniform and the way my body looked in it. Veering away from the main strip, I'd pull out the packet of cigarettes I'd stolen from the carton my mother kept in the kitchen drawer and light one up. I always smoked at least two or three on the way home. I was never worried about getting caught. Like most seaside villages in England, the streets were narrow and it was easy to get lost in the shadows.

❣

This was around the time my father accepted another job back in Oman. I was desperate for us all to return with him, but my mother had done her dash with expatriate life. She wanted to be close to her sister and no amount of pleading could change her mind. We said goodbye to him towards the end of the summer, promising to write, and then he was gone.

My parents had never been what you'd call particularly 'hands on' when it came to supervision, and my father's absence made it even easier to roam the streets aimlessly. I began to walk a lot, packet of fags and lighter buried in the deep pockets of the practical waterproof anorak my mother had bought me when we'd first arrived. I'd discovered it wasn't necessary to risk stealing cigarettes from the drawer in the kitchen. This was 1994, and you could buy a pack of Silk Cuts for two pounds at the local newsagent. I told them I was buying them for my mother and they never questioned it.

I often liked to ramble through the lonely common across the way from our house. There was a lake in the middle with a semi-rotting bench beside it, and I'd sit there smoking, watching the ducks and posing in what I hoped was a moody fashion. Addicted to this new feeling of weary malaise, I decided to stop eating. While I'd struggled before to curb my appetite, I discovered that the only thing my confused teenage self found more satisfying than a full belly was a ravenously empty one. Instead of secretly scoffing chips, I fed off the thrill that came from watching as my body shrank and my clothes got bigger. The days grew shorter alongside the circumference of my waist, and by November I had managed to turn myself into a completely different person. These were the early days of heroin chic, when cheekbones sat like half-opened louvres casting shadows beneath dull eyes, and I'd nailed the brief. I was still a super nerd, awkward and shy around anyone even remotely cool, but the life I had aspired to no longer seemed so impossibly out of reach.

To celebrate, I bought myself a short, tight black skirt to wear to school, rolling the waistband up until the hem just skimmed the top of my thighs like I had seen some of the Sweeties do. I understood the full impact of the transition I'd made one afternoon in early December while wandering down the school corridor. I was heading to the cafeteria to buy a Diet Coke for lunch (in fact, it was the only thing I allowed myself to consume during the day) when I heard two girls whispering and giggling behind me.

'*Slut*,' I heard one of them say to the other.

I cracked the Diet Coke can open with a little more swagger than usual that day. And when I walked home through the cold, grey streets after school, I decided to stop in at one of the cheap shops in town to buy myself some bangles. They made a pleasing tune as they rattled on my wrist, and I reached for more food at the dinner table that night just so I could hear them jingling. Of course, I didn't eat any of it. But by then no one expected me to, so it didn't really matter.

❣

I spent the winter months that year working as a kitchen hand at a local nursing home. I worked three nights a week and all day Saturday, washing dishes and delivering food to the bedrooms of residents who were too frail to eat in the dining room. My frenemy Bree had got me the job. She worked the alternate nights to me and Sundays, and we sometimes compared notes on Eric, the elderly man in room three who always found an excuse to touch us on the bottom.

'Just make sure you never turn your back on him or get too close,' Bree had told me when I'd first started there. 'You can avoid most of it that way.'

I tried to keep the meal trolley between myself and Eric whenever I dropped off his dinner, but he'd often find an excuse to draw me closer, asking me to pick something up off the ground for him or pretending he was having trouble cranking the radiator.

When I mentioned it to the home's manager she laughed knowingly. That was just Eric, she told me. Old and essentially harmless. 'He's just a bit lonely,' she said.

Loneliness seemed to afflict most of the residents of the nursing home. Those who were still able to leave their rooms spent long stretches of time sitting in the recreation hall, waiting for one of two things that never seemed to come fast enough: families who visited them, and death. I learned not to grow too close to any of them, as it wasn't uncommon to turn up for a shift to find a bedroom being stripped down and cleaned. 'Oh, Margaret?' the staff might say when I asked. 'She died this morning.'

The only resident I really liked was a woman named Olive. She was a jolly, matronly type with a lovely round face and a big smile, and I always found myself chatting with her for a few minutes longer than I was really allowed when I collected her dinner tray. She rarely had visitors, which seemed a terrible shame, because she was really so nice. She asked me about school and my hobbies and told me how much she loved my hair, and she never asked me about boys, which saved me the embarrassment of having to confess that there was precisely nothing to report on that front.

I'd had very little experience of what you might call a kind of grandmotherly warmth, my maternal grandmother being decidedly unmaternal and my father's parents both excessively formal. But Olive always seemed thrilled to see me, and I suspect if I had crawled into bed with her and asked for a cuddle she would have happily obliged.

One night a week or so before Christmas, she stuck her head into the hallway and called out my name.

'I've got something for you,' she said, her soft face beaming.

I parked the trolley against the wall and walked into her bedroom.

'It's not much,' she said, pulling something out of her dressing-gown pocket, 'but I just wanted to give you a little something for Christmas.'

It was a block of Cadbury's Dairy Milk chocolate, and she had stuck a festive bonbon onto the corner. She must have asked one of the other staff members to buy it for her, a small but thoughtful gift for the shy girl who delivered her dinner three nights a week.

'Oh, Olive,' I replied, taking the chocolate from her. 'This is so nice of you. Thank you so much.'

I gave her a hug and she patted my back gently.

'Well,' she said, after a moment had passed, 'it's not much, but I just thought you might enjoy it.' She pushed me back to look at me, smiling. 'You're a good girl,' she said.

I thanked her again, then took the trolley back to the kitchen to wash up the remnants of the evening's dinner service. I felt sad, because of course I couldn't eat the chocolate Olive had given me. I gave it to my brother instead, tossing it at him when I got home.

Lying in bed later that night, I ran my hands over my protruding hipbones and felt a combination of relief and pride. I had passed some kind of test, proof of a willpower I'd been cultivating that had finally come to fruition. Somewhere wrapped up in it was a prickling feeling of guilt, a feeling that magnified when I turned up to work a few weeks later to hear that Olive had died in her sleep. But I pushed it aside and told myself that she would have understood. I was thin now, and that required certain sacrifices.

❧

I kept working at the nursing home even as the egg of winter cracked and a brisk spring emerged. Each night, I checked the weather report to determine what to wear the next day. I treated anything above nineteen degrees as practically sweltering, which made it acceptable to choose something from my growing collection of cheap, strappy singlets and crop tops emblazoned with slogans like *99% Angel, 1% Bitch* and *Don't Touch What You Can't Afford.* I wore them under my school shirt, unbuttoning it at 3.30 pm or sometimes taking it off completely and heading with Bree to the park in the centre of town.

The park was where the older boys congregated, most of them paired up with a girl in the year below me. These were the girls who'd developed early, girls with full lips and big boobs and names like Brooke and Hannah and Debbie. Some of them were rumoured to be having sex already, but it wasn't the same as being a slut because they were popular and these were boys who either loved them or at the very least liked them a lot. These boys had sex with other girls too, but as they weren't girlfriends it meant they weren't special and therefore didn't respect themselves. Even at thirteen, we understood this to be an important distinction.

Being only moderately pretty and closer in age to these boys than their twelve-year-old girlfriends, Bree and I occupied that peculiar state in which our presence was tolerated while not being enthusiastically sought out. We mostly sat together on the edge of the group, smoking and dutifully observing the boys as they lived—nodding when they said something serious, laughing when they did something that was clearly meant to be funny and shrieking in exaggerated horror when they did something disgusting, which was frequently. We never talked to their girlfriends and they never talked to us. Instead, they'd whisper and giggle with each other while occasionally shooting us glances that were sometimes pitying and sometimes just bored.

It goes without saying that the boys rarely talked to any of us, girlfriends or otherwise, preferring the company of each other and all that barrelling physicality. The raw intimacy of brotherhood that begins in kindergarten and seems to prevail throughout men's entire adult lives is especially pronounced in adolescence, and these boys were no exceptions. They'd pick their noses and flick the contents at each other before rolling around together on the ground to mock wrestle, each of them feeling I'm sure some kind of stirring in the loins that they hoped wouldn't announce itself unexpectedly. Afterwards, they'd disappear with their girlfriends, Brooke-or-Hannah-or-Debbie's face lighting up as a newly callused hand reached down to pull her up off the grass, letting herself be drawn into a close hug and steered into the shadows of the trees. Or, if the relationship was very serious, they might be walked home to bedrooms where the remnants of childish innocence—fluffy pink comforters and beloved stuffed toys stacked neatly against pillows—competed with the beckoning call of adulthood and all its furtive, visceral secrets.

After the couples had dispersed, Bree and I would share one final cigarette and then walk home, giddy with commentary about our respective crushes. She liked a boy named Andy, whose chiselled jaw and jet-black hair made him practically model-like this far north of London. Unlike the rest of the boys, he was 'between girlfriends'—but he paid her barely any attention anyway. We disregarded his obvious lack of interest, dismissing it as a sign of what was clearly his unparalleled depths. It wasn't that he didn't or couldn't like Bree; it was that he required more *finesse* than the other boys, whose desire we also craved but whose good looks we knew were not complex enough to unlock the various doors that lay between Sheringham, Norfolk and Potential Stardom, The World.

I indulged Bree for the appropriate amount of time expected before I was allowed to shift the conversation to my own crush, a boy named Will. I'd fallen in love with him a week or so earlier on the clifftops that overlooked the North Sea. We had all traipsed up there from the park, a couple of the boys carrying giant cans of lager in their pockets which were then cracked and passed around for everyone to take a sip from. I was still nervous in their company, terrified to make a sudden move for fear I would be laughed at and asked to leave. And so I sat on the edge of the circle, puffing on a cigarette and saying little save for a murmured *thanks* when the warm beer came my way.

Despite the change in seasons, it was still cold on the cliffs, with an icy breeze that sliced to the bone. I sat shivering in my midriff top and bare shoulders, clutching my knees to my chest and trying to conceal the sound of my chattering teeth.

'Are you cold?' a quiet voice to my left asked me.

I looked up to see the words had come from Will, a sandy-haired boy who was going out with Brooke-or-Hannah-or-Debbie and who, I was sure, must have spent some time underneath her fluffy pink comforter.

'Oh no,' I replied, smiling. 'I'm fine!'

I was freezing, but I also dreaded the thought of being an imposition to anyone (let alone *a boy*), a fear that I have carried through into my adult life.

Unconvinced, Will popped his cigarette into the corner of his mouth and proceeded to pull off his black Adidas jacket and pass it to me.

'There you go,' he said, smiling. 'You can wear it until we head back.'

He turned to rejoin the conversation, something about Oasis's new album or what everyone would be studying for their A Levels. Everything went on as normal, which seemed crazy to me given the fact my world had been turned upside down. The crashing waves and howling wind had morphed into orchestral music. The clouds had parted to bathe us all in sunshine. I felt like I was floating three inches above the ground.

I wrapped myself in the jacket and breathed in the heady scent of teenage boy: pheromones mixed with tobacco and the slight musk of armpits. I wanted to say something interesting, something that would make him laugh or think me a clever thing, but the cadence and concerns of these teenagers were still like a foreign language to me. And so I sat there as silent as before, and sensed perhaps the slightest amount of disappointment on his part that the quiet girl might just be boring after all.

Later, after the sun had all but disappeared and our shadows had merged with the twilight, I reluctantly handed the jacket back with another quiet *thanks* and a shy glance, and walked home alone.

I replayed the scene over and over as I went to sleep that night. His face in the golden light of the setting sun. The way the cigarette had dangled expertly in his mouth, the burning ember reflecting on the peach fuzz of his upper lip. He was a boy with soft features on the brink of being a man, and in that way it felt safe to let myself love him, to let my heart be broken by him, the way so many of us decide to when we are young and exploring edges over which we might fall.

❣

The warmer weather brought more tourists to the seaside town, families and couples beating the summer crowds to brave the pebbled beach and its still-icy waters. I remained determined to work at the Sweet Shack and so, on a pleasant day in late April, I returned to ask Roger once more if he was looking for staff.

He stood in the same position as always, leaning against the doorframe and sucking on a cigarette with the TV blaring behind him. One of his permanent Sweeties was behind the counter—not Donna, but a girl named Alex with dark eyes and a haircut that made her look like Winona Ryder. She was in my year at school, and we chatted occasionally after class. I'd mentioned to her how much I wanted to work at the Sweet Shack, and she'd promised to put in a good word for me.

She smiled at me as I walked in. 'Hey,' she said. She turned to her boss. 'Roger, this is the girl I was telling you about. She's looking for a job.'

Once again, he looked me up and down, his gaze lingering a little longer on me than it had the year before. I was wearing my school uniform, the tight black skirt hugging my hips and a thin white shirt unbuttoned down to the centre ridge of my bra.

'Got any experience?' he asked again.

I told him I'd spent the previous summer working at the ice-cream shop a few doors down, and that I could be ready to start whenever he wanted me. I pushed a lock of hair behind my ear as I spoke to him, the bangles on my wrist jingling.

He took another drag on the cigarette, pinching it between his stained fingers.

'All right,' he said, exhaling. 'Come in tomorrow afternoon and we can try you out.'

He turned back to the TV, but I could feel his eyes on me as I walked towards the door.

'See you tomorrow,' Alex said, giving me the thumbs-up.

I walked home feeling invincible.

❣

The feeling of invincibility had worn off by the time I stepped back into the shop the next afternoon. I'd taken great care with my 'first shift' outfit, changing out of my school uniform and into a short denim skirt with a tight t-shirt. It was what I'd seen most of the Sweeties wear themselves, save for Alex, who got about in baggy trousers, scuffed Doc Marten boots and a loose t-shirt. In a few short years, I would be dressing the same—although my impulse to disentangle myself from the tropes of femininity would come less from having harnessed the nonchalance of girls uninterested in other people's desire and more from the belief I had little right to claim it. For now, though, I was still trying sexy on.

Roger seemed happy to see me, which I took as a good sign. I'd be working alongside Donna, who was behind the counter already with her long hair pulled into a ponytail on top of her head. She'd carefully pulled out some strands at the front, and they hung in straight lines over cheeks that had a smattering of pimples across them.

'Hiya,' she said, nodding to me. We were in the same year at school but we hadn't spent much time talking. Despite the pimples, Donna was a girl with a preternatural maturity who seemed to have barely registered my existence outside of the two times she'd spoken to me—both of them while standing next to an ice-cream counter. In time, we'd come to be sort-of-friends, and I'd learn that what I'd taken for mocking derision was actually just her loud, sarcastic but generally well-natured disposition. I can still see her now, lean and long-limbed with slightly crooked teeth that bared themselves whenever she let out one of her big, braying laughs. Like most of the women I've been in love with throughout my life, I was both thrilled by her and incredibly intimidated.

That afternoon, though, she was cordial but cautious. Roger had a way of making the girls who worked for him feel territorial about his preference for them, or perhaps this was just the effect he very quickly had on me. I smiled at Donna and squeaked a *hey* back at her, accepting the apron she handed me and tying it around my waist.

Roger walked me through the shop, pointing out the Mr Whippy machine by the window, the gelato freezers ('Try and memorise all the different flavours, yeah?'), the fridge full of soft drinks and, finally, the shelf above the till where the packets of cigarettes were kept.

'Got any questions, just ask Donna,' he said to me, before resuming his position in the doorframe. He flashed her a toothy grin. 'Apparently she knows everything!'

'Fuck off, Roger!' Donna squealed, throwing a tea towel at him. 'Ignore him,' she said to me conspiratorially. 'He's a complete arse!' But she was beaming, and her good mood lasted the rest of the afternoon, which she spent chattering away to me like we were old friends. I listened intently and laughed when I was supposed to, but mostly I watched. There was an ease to her movements that I envied. The way she occasionally tucked the strands of hair behind her ears and then flicked them out again. How she leaped about the shop to reach for things, darting here and there, leaning across the counter or out the window with her cleavage on full display and her bottom in the air. She seemed unencumbered by her body, which was how I imagined it must be for anyone who'd always been thin. She was raucous and flirtatious and brazen, slapping Roger on the arm when he teased her or flinging her arms around his neck from behind as if she were going to jump on his back.

I listened and I laughed and I watched and took note of all this, especially the fact that Roger seemed to find it hilarious and charming, which of course I took note of most of all.

❣

My trial shift went well, so Roger told me I could start work properly the next day. We soon fell into a steady routine, with me working a couple of afternoons a week and a full day on Saturday. As the weeks went by, I grew in confidence and capability. It wasn't long before Roger and I had begun to engage in the same easy banter he did with some of the other Sweeties, a rambunctious humour that moved between ridicule and praise. I wasn't quite as comfortable with myself as Donna seemed to be, but I continued to practise flirting with him until it became second nature to giggle when he said something slightly bawdy or put his hands on my hips to move me out of the way when he brushed past me behind the counter, which was often.

Being a Sweetie felt like being inducted into a whole new world. All of the adults I knew treated me like a silly child—especially my parents, for whom I was beginning to feel more and more disdain. I came home one afternoon to find my mother holding a packet of cigarettes that I'd hidden in my dresser drawer. She demanded to know if I was smoking. I denied it, of course, and said I had been asked to look after them by a friend.

'Anyway, why were you looking through *my things*?!' I shouted at her, twisting the issue to make it about her invasion of my privacy and not the fact she was frightened of the distance I'd seemed to travel from her when she wasn't looking. Later, I heard her on the phone to my father, who was still working overseas. *She says they're not hers*, I heard her whisper fretfully. *I just don't know what to do!*

It was different in the shop, where I was trusted with a level of adult responsibility and where Roger talked to me like I was not a child but a young woman. I was flattered by his attention and the way he spoke to me about grown-up things. It was an attention I was unused to receiving, and I had the feeling once again of having arrived into a life I'd thought would always be off-limits to me. The sensation filled me with a warm glow that was only eclipsed by the romantic fantasies I had continued to have about Will.

I hadn't spoken to him since the evening on the cliffs, largely because I turned into a terrified mess whenever I saw him. But while I may have seemed like an emotionless husk on the outside, inside was a different story, one I documented fastidiously in my diary.

I say 'diary', but the journals of adolescent girls more commonly function as our own personal burn books. Target: our bodies, ourselves. In deference to this long-standing tradition, I had bought a nondescript A4 exercise book earlier in the year, and by June had filled page after page with an endless barrage of cruelty towards myself. I was fat, I was ugly, I was boring,

I was stupid. I had a body shaped like a saggy water balloon, a bloated duck. I was a tits-less freak with gigantic hams for legs and enormous buck teeth. I wrote all these things down and rendered them into drawings, allowing the practice to both soothe and sting me.

My biggest fear was that someone would read the deep secrets I poured into the diary's pages. The terrible things I'd said about my mother, about my sister, about myself. The lists of food and calories and body measurements I recorded each day with religious conviction. The horrible way I wrote about my friends, criticisms born out of my own insecurity and jealousy and, in some cases, a defence mechanism wielded in response to theirs. It could be hard to know which girls to trust and which ones to be wary of.

Bree and I hadn't been spending much time together, not since it became clear that she'd told some of the park boys about my crush on Will. I had no solid proof that this had happened, but I had known it to be true ever since the afternoon I'd walked past Will and his best friend Danny coming towards me on the High Street. My stomach dropped the way it always did around him, but there was something else in the air that day. A crackle of tension, the premonition we sometimes have that something terrible is about to happen, a slow-motion car crash in action. I steeled myself as they approached, and wasn't entirely surprised when Danny began taunting me in a singsong voice.

'Will Upton, Will Upton, Mrs Will Upton!'

Danny looked directly at me on the last repetition of this, cackling sharply and wrapping his arm around Will's shoulders to solidify the act of fraternal bonding.

I felt my blood run cold as my entire body turned to stone. They were still coming towards me, and our paths were about to cross. *Keep walking,* I told myself. *Don't react. Don't let them know that they've hurt you.*

I couldn't bear the thought of Will laughing at me, but when he told Danny to shut up and pushed his arm away, I flashed him a quick look. He glanced at me quickly and smiled, and it wasn't a trap or a joke. It was warm and kind, and in its brevity told me that even though nothing might ever happen between us, he didn't find me ridiculous or worthy of scorn for wanting it to.

They moved on, as the caravan always does. I walked home in the warm afternoon sun, my face rigidly still in defiance of the storm of emotions I was feeling inside. *Don't cry, don't cry, don't cry,* I kept repeating to myself. I was an ice castle by the time I got home, and I crawled inside the coldest of those rooms to curse Bree in my diary. *Bitch!* I scrawled angrily. *Stupid fucking bitch! Stupid jealous fucking stupid bitch!*

I damned her with every terrible word I'd ever heard, but the act failed to calm me. Instead I felt restless. It was another one of those quiet weeks at home, and my mother was still asleep. I knew she wouldn't emerge until just before dinner, so I put some lip gloss on and headed back into town, where I expected Roger to be closing up for the night.

'Back again, are you?' he asked as I walked in. 'What happened, did you forget your skirt?'

I looked down at the tight black skirt I wore to school and shot him an exaggerated look of disdain. He was grinning at me.

'Shut up!' I said, laughing. I walked over to the cigarette counter, hoisted myself onto it and leaned back against the wall.

'Just thought I'd come and hang out,' I said.

Roger had locked the door and was about to count the till, so I pulled out my cigarettes and lit up. He didn't mind if we smoked, as long as we didn't do it while we were working or in front of customers. He was cool like that.

'You know,' I said to him, exhaling a thin plume of smoke, 'I could learn how to close up here.'

'You reckon?' he asked, more than a hint of doubt in his voice.

'Yeah,' I said, swinging my legs down over the counter and brushing past him. Grabbing the broom, I started to sweep the floor while I kept talking.

'I mean, it's not like it's *hard*. I practically do it with you anyway. And I know Rebecca's going off to college after the summer, so she won't be able to do it anymore.'

At sixteen, Rebecca was Roger's most trusted employee. She was quiet and studious, but she had worked for him for a few years and earned fifty pence more an hour than the rest of us. I didn't think she was much fun, but as Roger didn't seem to flirt with her like he did the rest of us, I wasn't particularly skittish around her either. She was just Rebecca—sturdy, hard-working Rebecca.

'All right,' Roger said, pinching a cigarette between his thumb and forefinger and taking a huge drag. 'You can stick around until close tomorrow and I'll show you what needs doing.'

And from then on, I was on closes. It was that easy.

❣

I turned fourteen at the end of June, and to celebrate I had a sleepover. Since falling out with Bree, I had become friends with a small group of girls from school. They were nice and funny, concerned about doing well at school but not *too* concerned and, like me, they were inexperienced in the ways of the world. I felt as if I could be myself around them, which was a change from the pressure I felt in almost every other social environment.

We went to see *Muriel's Wedding* at the cinema and then headed home to gorge ourselves on chocolate and crisps while shrieking and laughing. I had a spirited debate about the end of the movie with my friend Jane who, despite being the wildest one of us, felt let down that Muriel hadn't ended up with Brice the parking inspector. I said she had missed the point entirely, and we argued back and forth until the conversation became tiring for everyone else and we moved on to discussing the important matters of the day—boys, school and how annoying our parents could be. Jane told us she'd lost her virginity to her cousin during a family holiday a few months earlier, and we pretended to believe her.

Afterwards, when everyone was asleep, I crept to the bathroom and purged all the food from my body. I was practised at this now, having recently mastered the art of regurgitation. Despite the willpower I'd shown regarding Olive's present at Christmas, I'd found I hadn't been able to resist eating the ice cream I served to customers in the shop. Overwhelmed by guilt and fear one afternoon, I kneeled in front of the toilet and brought every last bite back up until my chest was clammy and my eyes watered. I stared at the contents of the bowl and thought how easy it had been. I could do this again, I thought to myself. I could eat actual food and not have to worry about gaining back all the weight I'd lost, the weight that had made me so ugly and which my parents had disapproved of.

Of course, I was still careful. I saw purging as a way to magnify my strict diet rather than replace it. It seemed the key to the best of both worlds: I could continue to maintain the heady rush of control that denying my appetite gave me, but I could also treat myself occasionally to the things that other, normal girls were allowed to eat. And so that night I gorged on popcorn, peanut M&M's, gummy lollies and crisps, safe in the knowledge that it wouldn't be inside me forever.

We woke up the next morning, bleary-eyed, and indulged in the typical teenage girl activity of negatively comparing ourselves to one another. My friend Clare and I were especially obsessed with our bodies, and we were in constant competition to be recognised as the most hideous among our friendship group. We treated it like a joke of course, laughing as we compared arms and thighs. On this morning, we decided to settle the matter by measuring our various body parts. The intention was ostensibly to satisfy our claims of being more monstrously oversized than the other, but we each secretly hoped to be proven wrong. It was a strange joke, but it felt entirely natural to us at the time. The game ended when Clare declared in mock horror that her foot was 'fucking *nine inches wide!*' and we collapsed, giggling.

After they left, I took the tape measure out and assessed my body again. I had purged all the junk food in my system, but still, you couldn't be too careful.

❣

School broke up for the summer and I began working longer shifts at the shop. I wasn't upset about signing away my holidays. On the contrary, I enjoyed the increased level of responsibility I had been given. A couple of new girls had started to cover the summer crowds, and I took great pleasure in exercising a kind of managerial authority over them. One of the jobs I withheld from them was the distribution of sanitiser in the ice-cream scoop water.

'It's very delicate,' I told them one afternoon. 'Only me and Donna and Alex are allowed to do it.'

I enjoyed too the feeling of being one of Roger's 'top girls'. I was flattered to think we shared a special connection, and delighted in the moments when he expressed it publicly, like when a group of his friends visited the shop and he spread his arms in welcome while gesturing to all of us on shift that day and saying, *Aren't I lucky to be surrounded by so many beautiful young girls?* Or the time he crept up behind me when I was serving cigarettes to a customer and tiptoed his fingers up the back of my leg until he reached my mid-thigh.

'Roger!' I squealed, laughing and batting his hand away.

How glorious it was to be chosen! To feel the prickling of someone's approval like that—and a fully grown man's, no less. After one such incident, I found the courage to ask him a question while we stood out the back smoking. Donna's cousin Lisa was working the counter, so there was no need to rush back.

'Who do you think is the prettiest here?' I asked, fixing him with a look.

I hoped he would say me, but steeled myself to hear him say Donna. She was the obvious choice, I knew, with her long hair and wild limbs. Imagine my surprise when instead he chose Alex, the tomboyish girl with the Doc Martens and the baggy pants.

'She's my type,' he said, looking at me while puffing on his cigarette. 'There's something about her I just find really sexy.'

I nodded seriously, taking a drag on my own cigarette in an attempt to conceal the disappointment I felt inside.

'That makes sense,' I replied, feeling a mixture of sad and stupid.

When we finished work, I let Lisa talk me into going out and drinking a six-pack of cider with her. I called my mother and told her I was going to Clare's house to watch a movie, and then Lisa and I set off down the road. I listened to her gossip about this and that, and tried to push Roger's words from my mind. At the off-licence, we started talking to a couple of older boys and they came with us to drink and smoke on the rocks down by the sea wall. After a while, Lisa began kissing one of them while I grew progressively more drunk with the other. He was sweet-looking, with auburn hair and a smattering of freckles, and if he had seemed unbearably out of reach then I might have fallen desperately in love. But the adultness of the situation and what it seemed to invite intimidated me, and so instead of kissing him, as he perhaps expected, I simply leaned my head against him and drunkenly nuzzled his shoulder. He put his arm around me in a loose embrace and didn't press further, and we stayed like this while trying to ignore the gentle moans Lisa was making to our left.

I was grateful he didn't force me to do anything more, because the thought of him touching me made me feel sick. Of course, I would have let him, because that's just how things were done. When his friend described to all the boys in the park a few days later how Lisa had let him 'suck on her tits and finger her', I laughed along with everyone else and breathed a secret sigh of relief that it hadn't come to that for me.

A week or so later, Roger and I were closing the shop together when he invited me to go out for a beer with him. This wasn't unusual in and of itself. I was well below the legal drinking age, but the local pubs and off-licences seemed to treat this as more of a suggestion than a hard and fast rule, and I had already been served my fair share of pints that summer. But I'd never been out for a drink with Roger, and I accepted the invitation eagerly. I pulled my long hair out of its ponytail as he locked the door, and then walked alongside him towards the pub at the end of the high street.

I grabbed a table outside while he ordered our drinks, and sat there in the late summer sunlight feeling grown-up and chic. He returned with a pint of beer for himself and what was known as a 'snakebite' for me—half lager, half cider with a big slug of grenadine. It was treacly and red, and a sure-fire way to become inebriated quickly and cheaply, which, for us kids, was always the goal.

We chatted amiably for a few minutes until Roger shifted the conversation to boys and relationships. I told him I didn't have a boyfriend, and he seemed surprised.

'A pretty girl like you?' he responded, flashing me the grin I'd come to like so much.

I blushed.

'Nah,' I said, taking a gulp of the snakebite.

'Well,' he said, 'you should enjoy it now, because once you get married you'll never give it up for your husband.'

I protested loudly, saying of course that wasn't true.

'Sure it is,' he replied. 'My wife never fucks me anymore. Couldn't get enough before we were married, now she's frigid.'

I listened, thrilled at the direction the conversation was taking. I felt flattered to be trusted with such adult information, to be treated like an equal who could handle conversations like this. I knew Roger's wife had given birth to their second child a few months earlier; I couldn't imagine how hard it must have been for him with her so wrapped up in the baby. I wanted him to know I was on his side.

'That's *so* awful,' I said, taking another slug on the snakebite. I could hear the waves crashing on the beach behind me as the warm glow of the alcohol began to burn my cheeks. 'Do you mean she *never* has sex with you, ever?'

'Nup,' he said, lighting a cigarette. 'Anyway, she's a mess down there.'

I nodded sympathetically. He didn't have to spell it out.

'I just go to prossies,' he continued, pulling on the cigarette and looking at me.

At fourteen, my knowledge of sex workers was confined to the negative depictions I'd seen in movies and the casual jokes I'd heard other people make. His revelation aroused even more sympathy in me for his situation, and I was eager to support him.

'Gosh, that's awful,' I said, patting his arm.

'S'alright,' he said, lighting another cigarette and leaning forward to light mine. 'Anyway, how's your drink?' he asked, pointing at the dregs of the snakebite, which I'd almost finished by now. 'Let me get you another!'

While Roger went to the bar, I marvelled at how fortunate I was. After a rocky start, things were finally looking up. I had some nice friends. I had a great job with an excellent boss who liked me and trusted me, and who treated me like a grown-up. My feelings for Will were fading by this stage, replaced with a sense that something bigger might be waiting for me out there. I had never experienced the thrill of being picked by anyone before, and here I was being charmed not by a boy but by an actual *man*!

Roger returned with the drinks and commented on the sickly sweetness of the snakebite.

'You should try Pernod,' he said to me. 'We used to drink that when I was in the navy. Tastes a lot like ouzo.'

'Does it?' I asked, as if I knew what ouzo tasted like.

'Yeah. It burns going down but gets you drunk quickly.' He lit a cigarette, then paused for a beat.

'I've got some in the flat upstairs,' he said. 'You should come and try it sometime.' He was looking at me, a half-smile curving his lips.

'Sure,' I replied, after a second had passed. 'That sounds like fun.'

We made a date for a couple of days from then. His wife was headed to Norwich, he said, and she wouldn't be back until late.

❣

Breathe out. Release the tension in your body. Before we go any further, I want you to know that nothing bad happens to me. Not the kind of bad that you're thinking, anyway.

This is a story about the space that exists between two outcomes. The what-ifs and the could-haves. This is a story about bad men who convince you they're good, because they leave the decision of your unravelling up to you. This is a story about how you can, for years afterwards, talk about these men as if they're still your favourite people. How fun they were. How cool. How much they respected you. How they didn't force you.

This is a story about how what they leave you with is not shame for having been with them, but shame for having not.

Nothing bad has happened to lots of girls. But we still remember it anyway.

❣

It was light outside when Roger took me upstairs to the quiet flat. I had never been inside it before, even though I'd seen him come and go. It was small, and there were baby toys scattered around the living room, which was where Roger invited me to sit while he poured the drinks.

I took a seat on one of the faded brown couches and waited for him to return from the kitchen. The thought of spending more time with him had excited me initially, but in the isolated flat I felt something shift. A bubble of anxiety had formed in my stomach, and it split in two and then four and then eight and on and on until it was a fizz inside me. I felt the weight of expectation descend, and the sudden panic of being in a situation beyond my control.

I felt all this, but sat there in silence, trying to ignore it. I was mature. I could deal with this. *This is what you wanted!* I reminded myself. Wasn't it?

Roger came back with the bottle of Pernod and two full glasses. I gratefully accepted one of them and took a sip, hoping it would ease the tension I was feeling. When Roger took a seat on the couch opposite me I let myself relax. We were just friends, after all, and being alone with him in his flat was just as normal as joshing around with each other downstairs or sitting outside at the pub. There was nothing to worry about.

We chatted about this and that for a bit, and he poured me another nip of the burning liquid. My previously fizzy insides had settled into a soft goop, and I was just about to light a cigarette when Roger shifted the conversation.

'Why are you sitting over there?' he asked, reclining against the corner of the sofa.

'What do you mean?' I replied, the cigarette paused halfway to my mouth.

'You should come sit next to me,' he said, grinning.

The fizz returned, and I laughed uncomfortably. Instead of answering, I lit the cigarette and inhaled deeply.

'You're all talk, you are,' Roger said, laughing along with me, but there was an edge to his tone that made me feel exposed and childish.

'I am not!' I protested, my discomfort suddenly wrestling with the anguish so many of us have felt in ominous exchanges with men: the fear he would stop liking me.

'Sure you are!' he insisted, leaning back again and smiling. 'I bet you're too scared to even come over here and give me a hug.'

I tried to rally some courage, and told him that wasn't true.

'Prove it,' he said.

I took another sip of the Pernod, then carefully put the glass down on the coffee table. I stood and crossed the small space between us, bending down to put my arms around his neck. Keeping my body as far away from his as possible, I patted him awkwardly on the back then released him and straightened.

'There you go,' I said, knowing I'd failed whatever test he'd set for me. The realisation made me feel sick. I'd thought of myself as having become mature and worldly, but it turned out that I was just a kid after all. I felt completely out of my depth, and the shame of it crashed over me like the waves on the beach outside. I wished I was outside too, where there were people chatting and safety in numbers. But I was here, in this flat, with a man who had invested time and energy into me and had expected something more than this pathetic display of nerves.

Roger looked at me and drained his glass.

'We should probably go downstairs,' he said. 'The wife will be back soon!'

'Yeah, I should get home too,' I said, relief flooding through me.

I grabbed my bag and hurried down the stairs. On the footpath, with tourists and locals milling about, I suddenly felt silly for being so scared and was embarrassed anew by my lack of maturity. I gave him a huge smile and thanked him for the drink, hoping he would forgive me. But he never mentioned it again, nor did he ever invite me back upstairs. I had missed my opportunity. The knowledge made me feel both relieved and remorseful.

He still lives there, you know. A pillar of the community, by all accounts.

❣

Recently, I asked Alex if anything had ever happened between her and Roger. I felt sure I couldn't be the only one. But she told me that, no, he had never approached her in this way. She thought it might have been because her father was a police officer, well known in the town. Too much risk of exposure. My family had no roots there, and neither of my parents were around enough to be considered a threat anyway. I was a safe option, in that regard.

For years, I thought of myself as the one at fault that evening. I carried the shame around, compensating for it by praising Roger whenever I told the story of the Best Job I Ever Had. There were so many good things about my summer as a Sweetie, and I thought of it—and him—fondly for a long time.

I still do, weirdly enough. But more than anything, I think of who I was that summer with a compassion that has grown over time. I want to send love to that girl, struggling with all her might to discover who she was. She was insecure and shy, too shy to talk to the boy her own age who she loved, and yet in need of validation from someone, *anyone* who seemed to see her in a way no one else did.

I wanted Roger to like me. I wanted him to desire me, in the childish way I understood desire back then. My crush was gentle and innocent, and I viewed our flirtation as a form of practice for what would come later. I didn't expect to ever have to act on it, nor did I think he would ever want me to.

It was the kind of crush I would have a year or so later on a friend of my father's, after we'd left the seaside town behind and moved to Australia. This was the man who taught me to drive and ride horses when I was invited to spend the summer on their farm. He called me 'Red', for my hair, and teased me in a way that made it clear he understood I was just a kid, and I loved him for it. When the summer finished, I returned to Brisbane with a bruised heart and promptly fell in love with my English teacher, a man for whom I felt contempt until he introduced me to *Pride and Prejudice* and my feelings changed drastically. We talked about Jane Austen and literature, and although he must have noticed how I started doing my hair nicely for his classes and sat up straighter than before, he was always just my teacher and that's exactly as it should be.

I was drawn to these men because they stoked physical and emotional desire in me, but also because they seemed to pose less of a risk to me than boys my own age. Boys who might expect you to do things with them; boys who would feel no shame in abusing you if you didn't. I had thought of these men as safe; I thought that through them I would have the chance to *play* at being a woman while never being expected to follow through on actually *being* one.

People like to say that teenage girls can be very dangerous for grown men, but the opposite is true. The opposite is *always* true. Grown men are dangerous for teenage girls, because they so often choose to exploit a dynamic they have a responsibility to understand and to maintain—that teenage girls are still children, and while we may spend time in that ephemeral state testing out the edges of adulthood, we must still be protected from being cut by them.

We call it 'being groomed' because it feels good. So much of the experience of adolescence is the opposite of that, and those of us who are left to our own devices swim in dangerous waters. I was lucky that summer. Many of us aren't.

A vulnerable girl makes a tasty meal for a charming man.

❣

Breathe in. Wrap your arms around your body. Give yourself love. Before we go any further, I want you to know that something good happens too.

This is a story about the space that exists between how you see yourself and how other people see you. The different kinds of what-ifs and could-haves. This is a story about nice boys who become good men. This is a story about how you can, for years afterwards, talk about these boys as if they never knew you. How invisible you were to them. How you always fell short.

This is a story about how wrong you can be.

Something good happens to lots of girls too. And if we're lucky, one day we get to find out what it is, and it will work to heal something within us that we didn't know was broken.

❣

While I was writing this story, I decided to look for Will on social media. There was no romantic motive to it, particularly not after all these years. But as a writer, I live in a perpetual state of examination and memory. We are not only remembered by the people who love us most throughout our lives, but by people who have loved us fiercely at certain *points* of our lives.

And so I wrote to him.

Hi Will,

This message will come completely out of the blue. You won't remember me at all, but we went to the same school in the early 90s. I'm messaging you now because I've been writing a book of personal essays. There's a bit about you in one of them, and I thought you might like to read it in the way that it can be nice to have memories of our childhood selves shared by other people. Other people witness our lives in a way we might not be aware of, and carry those memories around to make us eternal in some way. I remember you as being a kind boy who quietly cared about other people, and I hope you've had a really nice life.

I attached some paragraphs about that night on the cliff and pressed send. I didn't expect to hear back, and if I did I wasn't expecting more than a few lines. But I was pleasantly surprised when his name popped up a few days later in my messages folder.

Hi Clementine,

Thank you for your message. You're right. This has taken me by complete surprise. I do remember you and I remember that night very clearly. I was very intrigued by you. You were a breath of fresh air. You seemed to have a connection with the world, albeit a silent one. My memories of my teenage years seem to be a lot clearer than some of the last decade. Perhaps because of the friendships forged, the feeling of freedom and thinking that we were all more grown up and worldly wise than we were. We were all just kids.

He shared some details about his life. He had travelled the world as a chef but was married now and back in Norfolk. He and his wife had a couple of kids. He seemed happy, and I was really glad for him.

I was also shocked.

I do remember you. You were a breath of fresh air. You seemed to have a connection with the world.

I had always thought of myself as unseen, storing recollections and memories for everyone else but largely forgettable to the people who fascinated me the most. Will had been present during a period in my life when I felt the most invisible and misunderstood—*especially* by the people whose love I yearned for—and yet here he was telling me that not only did he remember me, but that he had recognised something in me. Something I hadn't even realised was there yet, but that would emerge in later years and become a defining part of my character.

I thought about the girl I was then. How shocked she would be to learn that she would one day receive this gift—the gift of someone else's memories, preserved carefully for almost thirty years until they could be drawn forth, fine and fresh and as if no time had passed at all.

I thought also about the girl I wanted to be then. How amazed she would be to discover that she and I might have been the same person all along.

Early adolescence can be dangerous, but it is also frequently beautiful. We are all learning how to *be*, practising various versions of ourselves on each other. Sometimes, we practise on people who want to hurt us. Sometimes, we practise on people who want us to think the hurt they cause is our own fault.

But sometimes, without even realising it, the people we least expect catch a glimpse of us. The setting sun throws light across the cliffs, a brisk wind blows the dust from our outlines, a boy sees that a girl is cold and hands her a kindness. And maybe, without her ever knowing, he thinks about her too, and wonders what lies beneath a surface that manages to be both so osmotic and so impenetrable at the same time.

How tenderly this knowledge makes me feel towards us all, racing as we were towards adulthood, not knowing that monsters lie in wait wherever we go, be they under beds or in them.

We were all just kids, We sat there constantly on the brink of magic and possibility, with our cigarettes and our bangles and our secrets and our fears, and none of us had any idea how sweet we were.

But we will, one day. We will.

EVERY SINGLE MOMENT
OF OUR TIME

I

Sometimes we cannot tell one story without also telling another, even if they are seemingly unconnected, because one story could not have happened without the other. And so let me tell you about the summer I fell in love, twice. This is a story about the mistakes we make when charged with taking care of other people's hearts. It involves a lot of alcohol, a little bit of music and an appropriate amount of double denim.

❣

Billie and I went to school together in a smallish country town roughly forty kilometres north of Adelaide, but our paths never crossed back then; she was a couple of years older than me and attended a different campus. Billie was your quintessential High-Achieving Young Lady. A good student, active in the music program, adept at handling teachers and respectable enough to be entrusted with that most solemn of responsibilities: college prefect.

In addition to all these traits, Billie was also secretly *super gay*. Despite the fact the south campus seemed to be the only place within a fifty-kilometre radius that had even considered the possibility that girls could kiss each other without a man there to witness it, Billie remained firmly in the closet. In year eleven she had a boyfriend who used to copy out poems written by Tennyson and pretend he had composed them himself. She knew he hadn't—of course she knew—but she kissed him all the same. When you're a lesbian in a small country town, there's a kind of safety in having a boyfriend. Luckily for Billie, he was much more devoted to sport than he was to poetry, so she rarely had to spend any time with him.

I would have been content with a sports-mad boyfriend in high school whose schedule was impossibly hectic because, despite my endless romantic daydreams, the thought of actually *kissing* another human being absolutely terrified me. I remember flirting with a very sweet school mate at a party one night, but I drew back the moment he moved in for a kiss and excused myself, feeling suddenly nauseated and like I wanted to panic-vomit. Just the thought of his mouth on mine was enough to make my palms sweat, and not in a good way. It wasn't his fault.

Like I said, he was very sweet, and he was moderately cute in a non-threatening, floppy-haired, fifth-member-of-a-boy-band kind of way. It's just that I was completely repelled by the thought of even the most PG-rated of my sexual fantasies manifesting into reality. I went home that night and cowered beneath my bedcovers, replaying the terrible scene over and over and feeling that same suffocating nausea. *Kissing. Ugh.*

All of which is to say that Billie and I had a same-same-but-different experience of a regional high school in the mid-1990s, with sexual desires and confusions we were both hiding to differing degrees until the moment we could escape the suffocating country town of our adolescent origin and head to the Big Smoke. (Being Adelaide, this just meant moving to a slightly larger country town. But it was the principle that mattered.)

We didn't talk about any of this at school or share any of the vodka-soaked confessions that would come later, because it took another ten years for us to actually meet. Billie was a well-known jazz singer by then, having graduated from the University of Adelaide's esteemed Elder Conservatorium of Music. I had seen her once or twice from a distance, performing at festivals alongside the other members of her cabaret group, Bacharach In Black. Despite her diminutive stature, Billie was unmistakable in a crowd, due in part to the blinding whiteness of her peroxided hair and the fact she liked to style it in spikes that were glued in place with industrial-strength hairspray. On someone else, it might have had the effect of warning people away, but with her round cheeks, big green eyes and cheeky grin, she endeared herself to people like some kind of cartoon hedgehog.

As an aimless ne'er do well who kept myself in short order breakfast cooking by being a struggling writer, Billie was the most successful person I knew from the various catchments of kids I'd gone to school with. I was in awe of her. I couldn't have imagined a world in which our paths might cross, but life is full of wonderful surprises.

❣

With the end of a decade looming, Christmas festivities were especially ribald that year, and Billie and I were both booked to perform at an event catering mainly to queer women. It was called Cream Your Denim, and as the name would suggest it was essentially an evening of very louche cabaret held in a creaky old building with high ceilings in Adelaide's briny seafaring quarter. My friend Emily and I had carved out a very specific niche for ourselves around the traps by staging shows where we sang ordinary covers and injected them with single entendres and other extremely obvious innuendo. Emily was a legitimately talented musician and songwriter; I was a glorified karaoke artist whom most audience members fondly regarded as some kind of bawdy alcoholic. But despite my obvious lack of professional skills and anything resembling real talent, Emily and I had something neither of those things can guarantee—electric chemistry and terrifically good comic timing. And so we were often booked to perform our weird mating dance in front of audiences across the city, which is how we found ourselves making rude jokes on stage that night while half of Adelaide's lesbians whooped and hollered with gay abandon.

From memory, my contribution involved little more than wearing extremely revealing denim shorts and doing some kind of comically sleazy dance on stage as the crotch of them crept further and further into the folds of my labia, which may or may not have been part of the official remit. Billie had been hired to provide lascivious commentary as the MC, but I studiously avoided talking to her all night, partly out of deference to her position on the social hierarchy that had been established in my brain a decade earlier (in the curious way that time and memory works, no one will ever seem as mature and grown up to me as the people who were in year twelve when I was in year ten and there are *rules* for this sort of thing) and partly because I found her sexually intimidating. Instead, I just tracked her presence in the room. I didn't need to look at her to know where she was. Billie might be as tiny as a mouse, but she's the kind of person you *feel* before you see. My skin thrummed just knowing she was somewhere in the vicinity.

I assumed she was indifferent to my existence, and so I was surprised to discover a message from her in my Facebook inbox a few days later. She'd sent it on the night of the denim extravaganza, but I hadn't seen it yet. This sort of lazy approach to technological communication infuriates me now (who waits two days to reply to a text?!), but things were a little different then. Most of us had only recently transitioned away from flip phones, for crying out loud. Nobody's really sure how we managed to communicate back then, but I suspect it was via disgusting, perverted practices like 'having actual conversations on the phone'. It was a truly uncivilised time.

Despite the fact that I'd already left it unanswered for two days, I held off on opening Billie's message for a little while longer, allowing myself to relish that crackling space which exists somewhere between anticipation and fulfilment. I brushed my teeth, climbed into bed and scrolled through other people's posts for a few minutes, pretending to myself that I wasn't thinking about it even as a smile played at the corners of my mouth.

Finally, I clicked on her name.

I heard on the tiny grapevine that your catwalk strut was bang-for-your-buck standard, she had written. *Sometimes being the saucy MC at the back with limited vision doesn't pay . . .*

I might not have been the most confident of women or the most sophisticated of lovers, but I knew enough to know that as far as opening gambits went, this was unequivocally flirtatious.

I don't know about that, I replied, trying to be cool. *Jenn sent me a photograph and it's pretty . . . ferocious. Also, Olivia says there were times when it was touch and go as to whether or not my vagina would make an appearance. Your eyes were probably the most untainted thing in the room. I cannot vouch for your temperament, though. I suspect it may be on the salty side.*

I wasn't sure if she'd reply straight away or if she'd even see the message, but as I lay there in the dark and stared at the backlit screen of my phone for a few seconds more, I watched as the checkmark next to it was replaced with a tiny avatar of her face.

Message seen.

Three bouncing dots appeared and then another text came through.

The salty side? she asked.

Salty meaning risqué words, I texted back, that tugging smile now a fully-fledged grin. *I would hope you'd be all over those, Ms Reilly. Salty words include, but are not limited to: dastardly; short skirt; windswept; blousy; terrible; and delicious.*

Ms Ford, please be advised that my name is O'Reilly, she corrected me. *I like risqué words. I like flouncy, behooved, calculation. I especially love delicious. In every way, Ms Ford.*

I flushed as I typed back: *I prefer to think of you as last name Reilly, first name 'Billie, Oh!' Also, another good word is hootenanny. Also, tiptoe. And: rustling.*

And with that, we were off. We continued in this fashion over the next few days, texting each other from beds and cars and work and bars. The connection felt effortless and exhilarating, although we each had different reasons for feeling this way. I was in the middle of planning a permanent move to Melbourne, which made the remaining months in Adelaide feel ripe with possibility and fearless opportunity. I had the luxury of being able to embrace disorder, at least until I could cross the border and outrun it. Billie was similarly drawn to the allure of chaos and throwing caution to the wind, but only because she had already begun the process of outrunning her past. She had recently separated from her long-term partner, a woman she'd spent the better part of a decade with and with whom she also had a child. The split was acrimonious and painful for both of them, which is to be expected when a once-sweet love curdles slowly without anyone noticing the bubbles rising to the surface. Later, Billie would tell me I was the first friend she'd made in a long time who belonged only to her.

I like you with the devil's drink seeping from your pores, she wrote to me one night. *I've had two experiences of you now and both work for me. 1. Watching you dance on a catwalk. 2. Receiving late-night messages on this social networking site.* She paused then added: *Syrup. Honesty. Tranquil. Pumpkin. These are not risqué words.*

Billie still worked as a professional jazz singer and, this being December, spent most nights performing at corporate Christmas parties at the Adelaide Convention Centre.

The masses amaze me, she wrote, describing the punters who came to her gigs. *Normal people with normal jobs and yet abnormal amounts of patterned shirts and alcohol consumption.*

It was a warm Sunday night. I lay on the couch in my living room, the sound of cicadas drifting in through the open back door. I told her that I'd spent the weekend alternately drunk and hungover and had thus given myself permission to do nothing that day except eat delicious food and watch *Anne of Green Gables*.

No patterned shirts, I replied, *but there was an impressive collection of complicated hairdos.*

Anne of Green Gables is sensational, she responded. *I do believe she was my first serious girlfriend.*

I told her that 'pumpkin' was one of my favourite words, and also one of my favourite soups. I told her I had been to a music fair the day before and bought a record of her namesake Billie Holiday's original recordings plus a large number of Greatest Hits albums because I enjoyed annoying music purists with the audacity of my basic tastes. I told her I had recently quit smoking and had taken great pleasure that weekend in feeling pious about it.

Such actions could probably be described by words like pugnacious, incorrigible, provoking and supercilious, I wrote. *I also think the sound of the word 'bucolic' lends itself well to this collection, except that it describes pastoral atmosphere rather than childish behaviour. Sometimes, I pretend it means the latter.*

This was how we fell in love with each other, in a way that felt simultaneously gentle and intense. We were like children, whispering our secrets into a tin can telephone, each clutching the receiver at our end of the string as we slept. It had been almost a month since she'd watched me precariously straddle the figurative (and literal) denim divide that separated my nether regions from the world, but we still hadn't met properly in real life. I liked that our friendship was being nurtured quietly and with intention, a fertile bed of soil in a secret garden being watered steadily each day while the roots of something magical took hold.

❣

Her parents were both Anglican priests, and she liked going to Midnight Mass on Christmas Eve. She messaged me shortly after the service had finished.

Someone read from the pulpit. They said 'impiety'. How righteous.

I'd had a gig with Emily that night at the Wheatsheaf Hotel, a whisky den in Adelaide's inner west beloved for its lack of pokies and abundance of handsome lesbians. Much like my first encounter with Billie, I had worn a pair of extremely short shorts. I told her about both the gig and the shorts, knowing she would be impressed by both.

I don't think the priest would have liked it, I wrote. *There was a lot of impiety.*

Despite the fact she'd seen me sing before, she was surprised to learn I did this in any kind of ongoing capacity. She replied immediately, demanding to know the name of my band and what kind of music I played. I was forced to correct her, advising that I was a 'singer' in much the same way I was also a 'dancer'— ridiculously, and for comedy more than anything. I told her I performed alongside Emily, who I described as being a Proper Musician.

She is the talent and the brains. I am the potty-mouthed sideshow she humours occasionally. I've tried to play an instrument but I have atrocious rhythm. I can't keep in time, even with myself. My eventual plan is to construct a band made up entirely of unrhythmic souls like me who'll play children's toys like the kazoo and battery-operated tambourines. We'll move to Berlin and call ourselves Malarkey Park and the Clunky Bunch. My other eventual plan is to gather some talents and start a 1960s girl group. But I think the first one will sell more t-shirts.

She laughed, or at least that's how I pictured it, and told me she thought the second option was a better idea. I liked to make her laugh. I liked making her laugh almost as much as I liked rereading my messages to her and imagining receiving them myself. I enjoyed thinking of myself through her eyes, impish and mysterious, appearing and disappearing without warning in the forest we had created for ourselves. Riddle me this, Billie. Riddle me *this*.

We went to the same school, you know, I wrote to her shortly after Christmas.

Another astonishing revelation! she exclaimed. *I have scattered few memories of that time. It was not my heyday, as they say. Were you a prefect? I hope so.*

I recounted the tragic tale of how my homeroom teacher removed my name from the prefect voting list because of my frequent 'tardiness', and she was gallantly sympathetic. I remembered her as a college prefect, and asked her what it had been like.

It was stupid, she wrote, which disappointed and thrilled me in equal measure. She did agree that the yellow piping college prefects were allowed to wear on their blazers was very fetching.

I thought about Billie often throughout the day, wondering what she was doing, and collecting absurd stories to tell her like a bowerbird rummaging for shiny scraps in other people's garbage. We had discovered early on that we both enjoyed the everyday kismet of glancing at a digital clock to see the numbers were all the same, and we'd started messaging the time to each other whenever it happened. (Rule 1: It had to be a truly random discovery and not something you anticipated. Rule 2: You had to text the time to the other person while the numbers were still identical in order for it to count. My favourite was 1:11. Hers was 4:44.)

Amazingly, we still hadn't arranged to meet in person, even though it had been weeks since she'd first messaged me. It didn't come up until the night we shared (no doubt) slightly exaggerated stories about how horrendous our school years had been.

What are you doing for New Year's Eve? she asked after I'd told her about the particularly crushing humiliation I'd suffered at the year ten social. *I have a show at the Convention Centre, but perhaps we could have a sneaky champagne afterwards or at the Wheaty? I often go there after a gig with one of the dancers I work with.*

It was a forward invitation insofar as it specified a date, time and actual activity. (Years later, as I wrestled with the tedium of internet dating apps, I would come to appreciate how rare such a thing was. These days, people are more likely to throw out a dull, *Up to much this week?*—my most hated question ever!—by way of sounding out availability for potential dates. The end result of this repetitious circling of the point is that no one meets anybody, instead just batting vague scheduling enquiries back and forth until someone abandons the conversation, perhaps having died from boredom.)

But I didn't understand any of this back then, and I was noncommittal in response. So noncommittal in fact, that I ignored the suggestion altogether. The thought of transitioning from the easy rapport we'd developed into something that might turn out to be as messy as it was thrilling made me feel as nauseated as I had at seventeen, when poor Travis Whatshisface had mistaken my flirting and hand holding for *flirting*-flirting and hand *holding*-holding and leaned in for a *kiss*-kiss. I adored Billie as a series of words on a phone screen that could be held at a safe distance, but I was terrified by the thought of Real Life Billie who wanted me to drink sparkling wine with her at a bar.

It wasn't just Billie. My tendency to cold-shoulder prospective suitors has been a constant theme in my life. It's too simplistic to reduce it to commitment phobia, although I've often jokingly referred to it as 'repulsion disorder'. It's the Groucho Marx theory of dating: 'I refuse to join any club that would have me as a member.' Oh, you like me? What a fool you must be!

But perhaps that's not quite the truth either. Maybe it's as basic as admitting that I don't like being responsible for other people's feelings. If you resist all expectations, you'll never let anybody down. If people like you, they'll figure out soon enough all the ways they can un-like you. It's a bit like Cher Horowitz from *Clueless* assessing the merits of a Monet: 'From far away it's okay, but up close it's a big old mess.'

I liked the safe distance I maintained with Billie, the liminal space in which she felt constantly charmed by me and in which intimacy could be constructed purely through bon mots and witticisms, and never anything resembling obligation or, worse, reality.

And so I said nothing, and she let the non-answer slide in her light, easy way. I poured myself another glass of wine and put my phone aside, where it remained silent for the rest of the night.

❦

I didn't hear from her again for a day or so, when she contacted me to tell me she'd listened to a graveyard shift I'd done on talkback radio. It was the morning of New Year's Eve, and I still hadn't responded to her invitation to meet her later that night for a glass of wine.

Things I have learnt about you from the radio, she began. *Student newspaper, editor. Column in the paper, but not anymore. Sorry to hear about your mother. You have a brother. You have a sister. You get The Monthly. You're a feminist. You love Barry Manilow. You don't like racists. Christians are a tricky bunch. You are very concerned about macular degeneration.*

She paused.

There are other things I'd like to know. But they are not appropriate topics for me to call in and ask you about.

Another pause.

If you're in town tonight, come to the Convention Centre. I'll sneak you and your posse in and you can dance to me and a twelve-piece band, two sexy dancers and three other singers. But watch out at midnight. The common people like to slobber all over the nearest moving object. I recommend standing very, very still. Or seeking me out. Let's flirt.

I waited until the afternoon to reply.

I slept until 3 pm. It was delicious, and a very clever way to avoid the heat of the day. At 6 am, I was a mess of delirium. However, I did learn that Branwell Brontë died standing up (in an attempt to prove it was possible to die standing up) and also that the universe is beige. I am cooking dinner for my recently ex-ed friend tonight and then possibly drinking champagne in my backyard. I shan't be able to make it to the Convention Centre, as tempting as it sounds to be both slobbered on and entertained by a certain wildly talented young lady.

After a moment, I sent a second message.

I enjoy flirting. Flirting is good. I am not very good at everything that comes after flirting, unfortunately. If I could live my life entirely through the written word, I should perhaps be far more successful.

I pressed send, and then typed: *Also, I was definitely assessing whether or not I have macular degeneration and onset blindness. My hypochondria is alive and well.*

A joke. To soften what I had said but not said.

In my living room, I used the eyes that had always caused me so much anxiety to track dust as it danced through the sunlight that streamed in through the window on the last day of the year.

'I'm sorry,' I whispered into the tin can.

'I understand,' I heard her whisper back.

I worried what my confession would do to us. But over the coming days and weeks, we held on to the cans and kept them warm with breath, sobs and laughter, and other signs of life.

And outside, the secret garden still bloomed.

❣

Billie and I became lovers, but not lovers in the way people have always understood lovers to be. Early in the new year, we finally arranged to meet. I was nervous. Although I had gently retreated from the idea of physical romance between us, I still wanted to impress her. I felt the same flutter of anxiety that preceded any first date, except the stakes this time were even higher. If she decided the *idea* of me was better than the reality, if I failed to be as funny and dazzling without the written word to hide behind, I would have lost what I already knew had the capacity to be one of the most meaningful friendships of my life.

I needn't have worried. Because this is what people don't realise when they dismiss friendship as a lesser version of romantic love: when you close the door on sex with someone, you find in its place an entire structure you hadn't realised was there, rising up out of the foundations you'd built. Suddenly, there are entire rooms to explore, windows to throw open, kitchens to sit in and sofas to slouch on. Sexual intimacy exists in a tiny space, a cramped flat of a shared life in which everything lives in such close proximity that you can never zoom out to see what your world could look like. Platonic intimacy is more liberating, less restrictive. Oh, the places you will go!

And Billie, as it turned out, would never have been tragically disappointed by me sidestepping her flirtatious invitations because Billie was already nursing a wounded heart the night my camel toe and I drunkenly sashayed down that runway. It wasn't the break-up of her long-term relationship that had done it; like so many people who choose to leave partners, she'd already worked through all of those emotions long before she packed her bags and walked out the door. Billie was broken-hearted over Sexy Straight.

Sexy Straight was a singer and occasional DJ. She worked at a nightclub Billie and her band liked to drink at after their own gigs. Billie fell for her immediately, straight women being like catnip to her. She has a remarkable success rate with them too. I've often thought to myself that women who think they're straight just haven't met Billie O'Reilly yet (or my friend Elise, but that's a story for another time).

Billie and Sexy Straight embarked on a passionate love affair that ultimately ended when Sexy Straight asked Billie to promise she would love her forever.

'Here's what I can promise you,' Billie told her. 'I promise that I will love you for every single moment of our time.'

I can understand why Sexy Straight was asking the question. At the time, she would have been thirty years old or thereabouts, and she'd only ever been with men. It's a generalisation, but most marketably beautiful women who've only ever been with men seem all too often to understand relationships as a linear proposition. We meet, we fall in love, we marry, we have babies, we grow old together. What can you promise me, if you can't or won't promise me forever?

Billie's inability to promise Sexy Straight the forever that she was so determined to lock down ultimately drove a wedge between them, and their relationship combusted in a fashion that was both spectacular and heartbreaking, particularly for Billie.

'Clementine,' she would say over the dozens—perhaps *hundreds*!—of glasses of cheap sparkling wine we drowned ourselves in that summer, 'I really did love her.'

'She was a shunt,' I replied one night.

Billie laughed, open-mouthed and joyfully, the way I always wanted to make her laugh.

'A shunt?' she repeated. 'What do you mean by that?'

'I just made that up,' I said to her, 'but it's exactly what it sounds like. An entitled, infatuated straight girl who likes the idea of a relationship with a woman but only if she can still play the girl.'

Unfortunately, Billie was terribly drawn to 'shunts'. It became shorthand between us for the kind of relationship we would never have with each other.

'I will never be your shunt, Billie O'Reilly,' I'd say to her over second and third bottles of sparkling wine at the Wheatsheaf.

'I would never want you as my shunt, Clunge,' she'd reply, using the nickname she'd christened me with one night when I'd recreated some scenes from the coming-of-age sitcom, *The Inbetweeners.*

She wrote a song for me and invited me over one afternoon to hear her play it.

'*Clementine,*' she sang to me, her fingers moving deftly over the keys of her piano. '*Thank you for teaching me how to say no/and you said no too/and now there's a chance that I won't lose you.*'

'You could never lose me, Billie,' I replied.

II

During the Summer of Shunts, in an entirely unexpected turn of events, I started seeing someone. He worked as an editor at a small publishing house in Adelaide, and I'd met with him one day to discuss doing some freelance work. I didn't expect anything more than a professional interaction, but over a single cup of coffee it quickly became apparent that we shared an immediate and electric attraction. Although it remained unspoken, by the hour's end it seemed we had both accepted that something would occur between us and we casually arranged to meet again to 'catch up'. I left in a heightened state of awareness, every sound around me magnified, the scent of flowers almost overpowering. Something significant had occurred. I couldn't explain it, but I knew from past experience that moments like that don't come along every day. It was a classic meet-cute, and all that was left was to wait for the rest of the movie to unfold.

We acknowledged our mutual attraction a few nights later, during a series of flirtatious texts. (Always with the texting! How on earth did anyone ever get together before phones lubricated the masses?) The conversation strengthened the certainty that we were about to embark on *something* together, something significant. I've only experienced this sense of romantic inevitability a handful of times in my life, but it's powerful magic, the kind that makes you believe in fate, meetings orchestrated by the hand of God Herself, the fact that there might just be such a thing as the One . . . or at least *a* One.

Some hours later he asked me if I wanted to stop texting and just meet for a walk, but the intensity of the situation was a little overwhelming for me and I declined. As I said, I've never coped well with navigating other people's expectations, especially not when they involve sexual desire or emotional vulnerability, but it's even worse when I feel the same way. Knowing that someone *like*-likes me feels both terrifying and suffocating, especially when I like them back. It's not just about the risk of being hurt, although of course I experience the normal human reluctance towards having my heart fed backwards through a mincer. It's also about the fear of stepping out from behind the curtain and the costume and showing them something real. I was raised by parents who, for better or worse, made a point of teaching their children that we should only speak to people if we had something interesting to say. On the nights they held glamorous dinner parties, my siblings and I would sit in the shadows at the top of the stairs and gaze through banisters at people who drank too much and smoked and laughed and gesticulated wildly while dressed in ruffled polyester and open-necked shirts. We were always forbidden from entering this secret adult space, having been reminded earlier in the evening that we could come down to say goodnight but no more than that because 'we love you but no one else is interested in what you have to say'.

The regular reminder contributed to the growing sense of social anxiety I felt about the space I took up in the world, and who would and would not consider me worthy of sharing it with. People could only be expected to show an interest in you if you dazzled them. Mastering charm is easy, but it's impossible to maintain. No one can be dazzling all the time, so it's imperative you prevent people from seeing you in your naked, boring moments. If you let the mask slip, even for a moment, people would have no choice but to turn their backs. Presumably to vomit.

It was summer in Adelaide, hot and dry and still. I suggested that we meet the following Saturday instead and go to the beach, and he said he would pick me up after lunch.

He arrived in an old kombi van that had been . . . well, I won't say *beautifully* converted for camping but at least *comfortably*. There was a deliciously nervous excitement between us, and we laughed and flirted gently as we drove towards the glittering ocean. I was relieved to discover that the conversation was just as easy in person as it was in text format, writing having always been a convenient shield to hide behind where matters of my heart are concerned. This easiness continued throughout the whole date, from a lengthy walk along the river that led to the sea and then as we bobbed around in the waves together. We were both in a state of heightened sensitivity, aware of the close proximity of our limbs beneath the water's surface. Our feet brushed against each other once or twice, and although neither of us remarked on it, the energy between us became further charged.

Is there anything more erotic than the moments in which some part of your body briefly and wondrously glances against that of the person you desire? The gentle knocking of knees beneath a table, the brushing of a hand against someone's fingers, a glimpse of the sliver of skin beneath a rising t-shirt as they lift their arms to pull a jumper over their head . . . this is the stuff lust is made of. Some people want kissing and fucking and grabbing and biting. Give me tension and tantalising distance and I will be yours forever.

We drove home in the late afternoon sun and mused on what the future held for us. There were no questions about if, only when. He imagined out loud scenarios in which we'd drive into the wild for camping trips, me reading out loud to him from the books we both loved. At night, we'd sit beneath the stars and drink wine until we were warm from the alcohol, then fall asleep together in the back of the van or even outside in the cool of the night air. I watched him as we talked, his face naturally warm and open, his hand casually resting on the van's gearstick. I could see the salt patterns that had formed on his cheeks, translucent silver creeklines running against a landscape of tanned skin. He glanced at me and smiled. I noticed that his two front teeth were ever so slightly crooked, and I fell a little bit in love with him right there and then.

We pulled up outside my house and looked at each other, suddenly shy. I knew he needed to leave fairly quickly, as he'd told me earlier that he'd arranged to meet some friends for dinner. The van's engine was still running, and the gentle purr of it seemed to match the current running through the air.

'I'm not going to kiss you,' he said, 'because I think once I do I'm not going to want to stop.'

Despite the tension of the day (and in fact the entire week preceding it), it was the first time either of us had spoken our desire out loud.

'That's okay,' I replied, smiling at him. 'I'm happy to wait.'

We hugged, the tiny fraction of space between our bodies holding an entire universe of possibility. I went inside, my cheeks pink and warm from the sun and the thrill and the attraction, but also from the *relief.*

For the first time in a long while, I was experiencing the blissful absence of romantic anxiety. It's hard to explain, even now after so many years and lovers have passed, but it just felt *ordained* in some way.

I spent the rest of the night daydreaming about him, replaying each moment of our date in full technicolour glory. Like all good daydreams or recollections, I slowed myself down when I got to the good bits. I knew you could rub too hard on the silver, overshooting the sweet spot and taking the shine away. The trick with a good daydream was to regard it as if you were watching from offstage and not the front row.

And so I watched us both from the shadows of stage left, and I was pleased with what I saw. Gone was the dreadful insecurity I usually experienced around men I liked. I didn't scrutinise my conversation for moments of accidental stupidity or the slightly too high-pitched exclamations I released when I was excited about something. I didn't feel ashamed of the fact there were things I *felt* excited about, and I didn't worry that he would find these things insufficiently cool. I didn't fret over whether he thought I looked repulsive in a bathing suit or wonder if looking at me at all inspired a level of disgust registering anywhere from 'mild' to 'extreme'. I didn't feel boring or pointless or ungainly the way I'd so often allowed myself to feel before with men, some of whom were just as great as him but most of whom were less so. Instead I felt confident and assured, like I'd finally graduated into some version of womanhood that had always seemed impossibly out of reach.

I was experiencing what my friend and soulmate Alice would probably refer to now as a great unburdening. All this time—an entire lifetime, it seemed; multiple lifetimes—I had felt myself to be *waiting* for something to begin. And here it was! Beginning! It didn't even seem like I'd had to work that hard for it;

I'd had only to be in the right place at the right time. I had been stumbling along for years, from the awkward and demoralising days of adolescence into an adulthood that hadn't felt any less complicated or confusing, but here it was: a life being presented to me, at last.

❣

The next day, I headed to a local park for a start-of-season barbecue with my roller derby league. He and I had been texting pretty much nonstop since he'd dropped me off at my house, and I asked him if he wanted to come and join us. He told me he would be there in thirty minutes and asked if he could bring anything.

This was a good sign, I thought. Not just the enthusiasm (which was a nice counter to the noncommittal approach common to so many members of my generation's lonely hearts club) but also the generosity of spirit on display. My first great love had never thought to bring an offering with him when he joined me at social gatherings. Nor had he ever thought to ask if I needed anything. He'd barely consent to drinking anything other than water when we met friends at the pub, because he considered it far more economical to pre-load at home first.

(Sidenote: If you're thinking to yourself there's nothing less appealing than a man who resents buying a bottle of wine to share with his girlfriend, you'd be wrong. There are plenty of things more unappealing than that, not least of which is the man who:

a) resents buying a bottle of wine to share with his girlfriend (you), but;

b) is more than happy to enjoy the one you've bought; and

c) who will, in fact, have helped himself sufficiently to said bottle(s) the night he strops off after a charity quiz and winds up pressing a woman you vaguely know up against a wall in an alleyway and fingering her while she moans into his mouth, the mouth now stained with the acrid tannins of the cheap red wine *that you bought.*

Of course, this will all occur only a few weeks after your mother has died, and only a few months after you'd told him you were pregnant and he responded by placing as much distance between the two of you as was humanly possibly while still being able to reach out and clap a hand on your shoulder and say, 'I'm sorry,' in the sombre tones of a man suddenly aware of the importance of good-quality barrier protection. But that is a story for another time.)

As promised, he turned up thirty minutes later with a dozen beers and an enormous smile plastered across his face. He was affable and charming as I introduced him to everyone, and when we sat on the grass a moment later it was with the easy intimacy of two people who wouldn't fret about the proximity of their limbs to each other because their limbs would already be touching and it would be okay.

It was heading towards late afternoon at this point, but the sun wouldn't set for a few more hours. I basked in the warmth of both the summer heat and the fizzy liquid that seemed to have replaced the blood in my veins. I felt nervous, but not in the way that I had so often been when dealing with men throughout my life, when you fear saying the wrong thing and being either misunderstood or, worse, exposed as inherently un-female in some essential way and therefore no good for anything at all. These nerves were different. Their threat was delicious rather than terrifying, like the feeling of anticipation when you prepare to jump, screaming and laughing, from a cliff edge into deep, cool water below. I saw him floating down there, beckoning to me. All I needed to do was close my eyes and fall.

The shadows had grown longer by now and those of us left sitting on the cooling grass made plans to go to the pub. I needed to use the bathroom quickly, and told him I'd be back in a few minutes. But when I began to head back across the oval from the small brick outhouse on the edge of the park, I saw that he was walking towards me.

'Hi,' he said when the gap between us had closed.

'Hi,' I replied, smiling, reaching for his hand.

He kissed me softly, for the first time, and I kissed him back.

Billie was at the pub when we arrived some time later, and I went to give her a hug. I'd told her about him, and was both excited and nervous to introduce the two of them. She was pleasant and vibrant, ever so slightly louder than normal (which was already loud) and overly familiar in the same way I can be when I'm performing a version of myself to someone I either want to be liked by, or to whom I want to make one thing clear: *you will never replace me, so don't even try.*

❣

I found out the depths of her dislike for him a few nights later. It was her birthday, and I'd gone to her house to drink wine and sing songs together at the piano. I'd told her I couldn't stay too late because I'd organised to go to his house for a sleepover. She had said that was fine, but both her temperament and her temper grew more boisterous as the night went on.

She had taken to referring to him as 'Lunch', a nickname she jokingly said was in reference to the Australian colloquialism of encroaching on one's romantic territory; i.e. 'to cut someone's lunch'. Whether she felt he was cutting hers or she intended to cut his was never clarified. Regardless, her disdain for him was combined with a sort of baffled disbelief that I could possibly find him attractive in any way, shape or form. As the night went on, Billie brought out more wine and jokes to bat away my every reminder about needing to leave until, after the fifth or sixth time I remarked that I should call a taxi, she at last turned to me with a look of hurt fury on her face and said reproachfully, 'Clementine, it's my *birthday*.'

I was a little stunned but not altogether surprised. I had felt the confrontation brewing since I'd first introduced them, when he'd become flesh made real and not an abstract character in the tales we told each other. I apologised for upsetting her but asked what exactly she expected me to do.

'Tell him you're not coming,' she replied. 'Tell Lunch you can see him tomorrow.'

'I'm not going to do that, Billie,' I said. 'I like him! Please don't ruin this for me.'

We were talking about a boy, but I knew we weren't really fighting about him at all. He could have been anyone, the only relevant point being that he wasn't *Billie*. And even though I had promised I would never be her shunt and she had declared she would never want that from a clunge like me anyway, I still could hear the whispered possibility of a what-if.

What if?

What if we could make it work, the balance of this perfect friendship with a more physical kind of intimacy? What if we could experience all of it together, and not need to choose one or the other in order to preserve the fullness of either? She was in love with Sexy Straight in the kind of robust, physical way that you can hold and scrape and bite and kiss and hoist and consume. But she was also in love with me and I was in love with her, and it was a different kind of love than either of us were used to. I made no demands on her and never would. I didn't need her to give me a commitment or the promise of a contract to last throughout our lives. The tin cans would always keep us together, and our secret garden would always bear fruit.

Sitting at the piano that night, I felt like I could offer her one of two things: a platonic life together that would stretch out far beyond anything we could see (especially me, with my anxious eyes) and always bring with it new things to talk about; or a love that would soon enough fade, taking with it the memory of all the things that had brought us together in the first place.

I have experienced this heartbreak a few times in my life. I have loved people deeply and enthusiastically, and yet known that the security of this love is contingent on keeping certain parts of it off limits, sometimes from the very beginning and at other times shutting them down without warning. Why not choose the path that allows you to love someone forever and be loved by them in return?

But what if, what if . . .

There was a hearth that still existed between Billie and me, the point where flames could either roar into life or slumber quietly as burning embers. It was the same place I'd find myself in years later with Alice, who I lusted after at first but then loved too much to risk loving fully, or whom I was perhaps able to love fully because I wouldn't, couldn't, risk loving her meaninglessly.

Thank you for teaching me how to say no. And you said no too. And now there's a chance that I won't lose you.

What do you do with a love like this? Billie had grown too important to me to destroy what we had with a physical intimacy that would only burn us both in the end. Some of love lives in the fire, and some of it in the steel guard that shields us from it.

Knowing which is which is the key to making both kinds last.

❣

I went to his house that night, the fight with Billie weighing heavily on my mind. It wasn't just her anger at me leaving. It was everything. The little jibes about his hair, the derisive nickname, her disappointed tone when she pondered my attraction to him. My desire for him and thrill at what we could be together had been like a story whose ending I had been in search of for years, but I could see its promise trailing away into nothing in the face of her disapproval. Even as I defended myself to her that night, I felt the magic of it all slowly leaking away, like the air in a sad, tired, three-day-old balloon. Sitting in the taxi on the way across town to his house, I tried to capture as much of the remnants as I could, to stuff it into bags and jackets and shoes and wallets and the pockets in the inside of my cheeks, a squirrel harvesting nuts for the winter.

Please don't ruin this for me, I thought again. Except this time, I was speaking to myself. Because the truth was Billie hadn't ruined anything. We love who we love despite what other people think. Billie's dislike had just made it easier for me to do what I always did, which was lean as far into empty space as I could without fully letting go, keeping hold of something behind me so I could pull myself back to steady ground the moment it got too scary. I had done it with so many people, liking them and encouraging their like of me, only to turn around and punish them for having feelings. I could try to blame Billie for my change of heart, but it was me. I did it.

By the time I climbed out of the car and knocked on his door, the excitement that had felt so precious and rare only a few days earlier had dissipated. In its place there was now a sense of dread.

He let me in, the smile on his face wide and sincere. He seemed genuinely thrilled to see me. I pitied him in that moment, because I already knew what was going to happen. I could see the inevitability of it as clearly as I had seen its potential. I should have said something then, voiced my concerns out loud or at the very least acknowledged the anxiety that was suddenly overwhelming me. But I was young, and still able to convince myself that if someone was silly enough to trust me with their feelings then perhaps they deserved everything they got.

He led me to his bedroom, which had a neatly made queen-size bed pushed into the corner. I sat on the edge of it and made a show of looking intently at everything around me. The high ceilings. The beige curtains. The plaster cornice around the light fitting. Anywhere but directly at him. I felt myself growing prickly and hostile beneath his gaze. From across the room, I could sense his eyes on me, and when at last I glanced up I saw that his expression was soft and blurred around the edges, a smile playing on his lips.

It was just the two of us in the house, but Billie's presence still loomed large beside me, so large that she began to fill the room. He sat opposite me on a desk chair, the kind with wheels and a bouncy reclining back and I found myself looking at him through her eyes.

157

Why did his *shorts* have to be that colour? And his *hair*? Weren't dreads something white men were supposed to outgrow well before they turned twenty-five? (To be fair, this is true.) He was rocking back and forth in the desk chair and I allowed myself to be irritated by the ugly practicality of it. Ridiculous objections, things no one could possibly think it was fair to criticise; the kind of things we reach for in order to justify our own disgust.

I could tell this different version of me was confusing him, and understandably so. Having engaged in some quite intense teenage make-out the night prior, we had—like teenagers—planned my visit with a very specific goal in mind: we were going to have sex. And until Billie had planted the seed of doubt in me, I had been looking forward to it! Kissing him had yielded promising results; like anyone making subtle reconnaissance on a prospective intimate partner, I'd made a show of rubbing my thigh against his erection the night before as a pretence of turning him on, but really I was trying to figure out what kind of dick he had. It's an inexact science, but I'd been fairly satisfied by my early findings.

Where was that eager girl, he must have been thinking, and why had she been replaced by this passive-aggressive scold obsessed with the decorative trim of his ceiling?

I told him I was feeling tired, and asked if he'd mind if we just slept.

Of course he didn't mind, and so we climbed into bed. I turned away from him, rigid against the light touch of his hand on my hip. If my attraction for him had been fading when I arrived, it had now disappeared almost entirely, replaced by a growing disgust for everything he was and everything he represented. Repulsion disorder had claimed another victim, and the rotting carcass of it loomed large in the bed between us.

I didn't want to have the conversation I knew was coming, the one where I was tasked with hurting his feelings and letting him down gently. And so I gave myself permission to hate him for it—to properly *hate* him—because he had committed the terrible crime of making me face up to the responsibility of ending things the way a mature adult might. How dare he!

I lay there and waited for sleep to come, and the promise of escape that morning would bring.

❣

The Summer of Shunts continued, and with it my rapid exit from the burgeoning relationship I had been so sure was the beginning of the rest of my life. Night after night, Billie and I would drink to excess at the Wheatsheaf and then pass out in my bed together, waking up hours later to the sickly sweet smell of cheap bottled fizz seeping out of our pores. *Never again!* we'd swear, only to repeat exactly the same routine that very evening.

Each time he messaged me, I'd roll my eyes and grimace, exaggerating the performance whenever Billie was there to witness it. My replies were short but jolly, the rejection of his repeated efforts to see me punctuated by excessive exclamation marks.

Oh! I can't tonight! I'm seeing a friend! I'm sorry!!!! Another time???

As break-up tactics go, it was an awful approach. Unkind, cruel, dismissive and utterly self-motivated. I assumed he would eventually get the message, but when he asked me straight out one night if I was deliberately avoiding him, I panicked.

'No!' I replied, because why would I possibly rise to the challenge of being a fully formed human being with advanced emotional skills when I could be a *fucking coward* about the whole thing?

'Then what's going on?' he asked plaintively.

Years and years after this conversation took place, I would start hosting a podcast offering 'frank, funny and feminist advice' to young women from the perspective of a big sister. If younger me had written asking for guidance on how to manage this situation, with the benefit of hindsight, this is what I would have advised her to say:

I'm sorry. I know I've been behaving terribly. It's not fair to you to treat you like this. The truth is, I find the prospect of experiencing intimate vulnerability with another human to be extremely confronting. Once the initial excitement wears off, I find myself overwhelmed with fear about what will be required of me to maintain an emotional and physical relationship with someone who has their own needs and wants and desires. Relationships have always felt like foreign territory to me, and self-esteem issues forged early on in childhood have proven hard to shake. To some degree, I find it difficult to understand why a person would like

160

me at all, and the fact that they do triggers my fight-or-flight response.

But none of that is your problem, and I'm so deeply sorry that I've made you the target of unresolved issues that I should really be working to heal through comprehensive therapy. Do you think we could try to be friends for a little bit and see if any potential for romantic intimacy could be built on that? Obviously I understand if you would rather not, and either way I would like to state how deeply sorry I am to have hurt you. You are a wonderful person, and you haven't deserved any of this.

This would have been the kind and mature thing to do. I've no doubt he would have accepted this explanation with grace. He was genuinely a pretty excellent person. Who knows? Maybe we would be married now with two or three children and a campervan named Betsy.

But we'll never know, because what I said instead was this:

'Nothing's going on! I like you and I want to keep seeing you, but I just don't want to do anything *exclusive*. Wouldn't it be great if we could date each other but also date other people?! Monogamous relationships are so limiting! Let's just be very French about the whole thing!'

A few things here.

First, monogamous relationships *are* very limiting. Writing this now at the age of thirty-nine, I have determined that 'non-exclusive dating' is precisely what I want for my life. But that's because I am a woman in possession of both a child and a heavy workload, and the idea of fitting in another person's long-term needs on top of that is, to be frank, vagina-shrivelling.

Second, if I'm honest, I still hold fast somewhere deep inside to the secret wish that I might meet someone who makes me toss away every last lofty, prattish thing I've said about non-monogamy and how it's the only practical way to function in a relationship. I am a jealous person by nature, my jealousy born of a deep insecurity. Why would they want you, when they can have—and *are* having, by virtue of the rules of non-monogamy you've embarked on together—literally anybody else?

Third, if I've learned anything since this period of regrettable behaviour, it's that honesty really is the best policy. Please see the aforementioned message suggested by my current self to the younger, more immature version of me.

Let me alleviate any concerns you might have that I've escaped punishment for treating other people's hearts with such cavalier disdain. I have suffered for my sins. I have had done to me exactly what I've done to others, and I have deserved every last wrenching sob, every ignored text and every overly cheerful excuse not to see me. I don't need to imagine how satisfying it was for Alice to see me experience myself exactly the same kind of confusing heartbreak that I inflicted on her, because she told me so in a conversation once as I was nearing my second hour of tortured whining about a boy who I felt had trapped me in his net and then, having found my scales less shimmery than he had perhaps expected, tossed me back into the sea.

'Oh, Clementine,' she said to me over the phone. 'I'm sorry you're hurting. It's very painful to be in such close proximity to someone who's made you feel this way.'

'I probably deserve it,' I admitted.

'That's probably true,' she replied, laughing. 'Still, I'm sorry all the same.'

But all this self-knowledge and self-awareness was still to come.

My obnoxious appeal to be 'very French about the whole thing' (calm down there, Brigitte Bardot) backfired, with the end result being the receipt of a handwritten letter spanning numerous pages. He would be thrilled to explore non-monogamy with me, he said, believing us both to be the kind of sophisticated bohemians who could handle the complexities that came with it. I think he imagined the two of us reclining in a literary salon, smoking cigarettes and engaging in passionate disagreements over books and ideas and people, each argument further heightening our inexhaustible passion for each other (which would sometimes include other people and sometimes not), whereas I have truthfully always been more interested in finding someone willing to eat crisps with me in bed while watching old episodes of *Survivor*.

I had already determined to hate every word he'd written because, as previously stated, believing him to be the one at fault here ('He's just too *keen*! It's like, back off!') was a foolproof way to completely absolve myself of any blame. On the final page, he mentioned a particular song that he felt best summed up our situation. He had downloaded it for me, he said, and saved it on a USB stick that was enclosed in the letter.

I picked up the torn envelope, fished around in the bottom of it and pulled out the USB. I plugged it into my computer and clicked on the little icon that had popped up in the bottom right-hand corner. There was a single file, and it started playing as soon as I opened it.

It was a romantic gesture, and I have participated in more than my share of those. I've written letters and posted them, hoping beyond hope that I had managed to charge them with a special kind of magic. I've searched for the perfect gift, the *just right* thing that will indicate a depth not just of feeling but of knowingness: I am a person who *sees* you. I've learned about music, movies, books—hell, even philosophy, which I *hate*—in order to turn myself into someone who might be seen in return. At university, I fell in love with a boy who had discussed with me at length his aspirations to be a film director, and who had given me scripts of his own 'for feedback'. I had read them all dutifully, offering adoring praise over rivers of cheap wine at a late-night pizzeria and then blow jobs under my bedcovers later on. I had written one of my own to offer him in exchange, wanting to show him I was a person not just in the world but a person in *his* world. But as I was getting into his car one night, I saw the once-crisp manila envelope into which I'd carefully placed the stack of papers lying crumpled and unopened on the back seat of his car.

'Oh, I haven't read it yet,' he said to me casually after I asked what he'd thought.

'That's okay,' I replied. 'It's not a big deal.'

I have injected all of this desire into my interactions with certain people, hoping that the *wanting* alone would be enough to lead us to our Hollywood moment: the resolution of the third act when they realise they've been a fool and they might be about to lose the best thing that ever happened to them. I have been victim to people just like me, crying hot tears at night wondering what it is I've done wrong and what it is I could possibly have done differently.

I've told myself lies to make myself feel better, the way we all do when trying to find meaning in heartbreak. *They're afraid to love. They've put up walls. They're confused by the strength of their emotions. It isn't that they feel too little, but that they feel too much. It's not that they can't love me, it's that they can't love anyone.* (To be fair, my first boyfriend said this last one verbatim as he broke up with me, which was about three weeks before he fell in love with a perky girl named Tessa.)

There's a reason this kind of thinking is fantastical nonsense. Because the strength of feeling, desire and optimism we feel for that 'what if' is something that belongs to us alone. And unless someone is asking to be seen and to be known and to be understood by you in the same ways that you are asking when you stand there and hand them a five-page script, hoping it will tell them everything they need to know about you and what you could be to them, then it's just a fucking envelope carrying a homework assignment.

All of which is to say: I didn't listen to the song on that USB stick the whole way through, and to this day I can't remember what it was about.

❣

Eventually, predictably, he grew tired of being treated with such disdain. Under the guise of being adults about the whole thing, we drifted into a kind of superficial friendship, which finally ended with a bitter fight over text. This part of the story is not really mine to tell, but suffice it to say he broke the heart of a friend of mine (sidenote: never date people in your industry, because you all end up dating each other). I responded very badly for someone who had done almost exactly the same thing to him, sending him a vicious message to which he replied in a similar vein, and at length. I won't repeat it here, but it included the words 'heinous', 'tumultuous', 'fickle' and 'bitch', all right next to each other and in exactly that order.

But within this (justifiable) explosion of fury, he wrote something else.

Don't presume to know me before you've so much as tried to understand me.

Amid the excavation of my life that has occurred while writing this book, the poring over text messages, the reminiscing, the reading of letters and thinking of moments that made me cry or filled me with deep, abiding shame, this is at least one clue to who I was and how I have conducted my relationships with people throughout my entire life.

I have spent so much time trying to *know* those people to whom I wanted to give my time, but so little time trying to *understand* them. I've assigned motive and meaning to their actions towards and feelings for me based on nothing more than my own assumptions, and in so many cases I have done the opposite of what I claimed to have wanted: I have made myself unknowable. I have kept myself from being known, holding people at arm's length because the fear of being seen in all my naked vulnerability—the naked *soul*, I mean, not the naked body—has been too terrifying to contemplate.

I don't know if I have the answer to this. Is it something you can consciously work to change? Can therapy do the trick? Maybe. But like all people who allow the membrane separating their exterior and interior selves to become hardened and impenetrable, I am fearful of change. It turns out maybe I'm the one who's afraid to love. What a cliché!

Six months after the Summer of Shunts, when the skies had turned grey and sodden leaves collected in the gutters on the streets, I packed up a campervan and moved my worldly possessions to Melbourne. One night shortly before I left, I met Billie at the Wheatsheaf for a farewell drink. She had moved across town, and we hadn't been able to see each other as much. I'd missed her.

When I walked in and saw her sitting at our regular table, I squealed in that gorgeous, high-pitched way young women (for I was a young woman then) do when they see their girlfriends.

Ohmygodhiiiiiiiiiiiiiiiiiiiitssogoodtoseeyouuuuuuuuuu!

'CLUNGE!' she cried, her vocal training leading her to enunciate every letter.

We hugged each other tightly, her platinum blonde head reaching to just below my shoulder, me towering over her.

That night, we drank endless glasses of the bad fizz and talked about everything and nothing. It was a cold, cloudless night and the stars twinkled above us like the bubbles bursting in our glasses. I was excited to start my new life, but I would miss so many things about the old one too. Riding my bike along the quiet, flat streets of Adelaide on hot summer nights, the temperature suddenly dropping as I sailed past the leafy parklands. The sound of the Central Markets on Saturday mornings. Raucous dinner parties at East Taste Cafe on Gouger Street, and the cheap box wine we consumed by the carafe.

And Billie. I would miss Billie.

When we hugged and kissed each other goodbye that night, she told me to drive safely and to call her when I got there. I promised I would, which seemed unnecessary considering we both knew I would text her at every pit stop along the way to share some observation or joke about the trip.

'I will never be your shunt, Billie O'Reilly,' I whispered in her ear, my arms wrapped tightly around her.

'I would never want you to be my shunt, Clunge,' she replied.

❣

Billie's married now, to a beautiful, vibrant country musician with a throaty voice and a temperament that perfectly complements that of my old friend. I went to their wedding, one of the very first to be officially recognised after same-sex marriage was legalised in Australia.

I cried, of course—good tears. She had found her person, the one she could know and be known to above all others. Billie had always deserved that.

As for me, I've fallen in love and then out of it numerous times. I've had my heart broken and broken hearts right back. What seems huge and big and all-encompassing at the time can so easily be forgotten years later, re-emerging only while excavating the grounds of another moment in history. As it is, I cannot tell the story of Billie and me without telling the story of a boy—but he could have been anyone, really. The important thing is that he, like all of us, was there.

Billie and I text constantly, mostly to send each other the time. Our message history is a long catalogue of numbers, sometimes with locations attached, sometimes sentiments.

1:11

4:44

3:33

1:11 (Blackwood. Seeing the bookkeeper.)

2:22

4:44 (Your favourite.)

5:55 (Emu Bay, KI. I'm on a dynamic detox retreat.)

2:22 (Flying to Sydney.)

10:10 (Lockdown. Sigh.)

When we speak on the phone, which is too rarely, it's as if no time at all has passed. The tin cans still work. Our last long conversation was about the man who had broken my heart, the one I had told Alice I'd deserved to be hurt by. I described the terrible feeling of having been considered briefly possible, and the yearning I had been left with to simply understand *why* he didn't like me.

'Clunge,' Billie replied. 'You're absolutely gorgeous and he sounds like a bloody dickhead. And he was shorter than you anyway.'

'You're shorter than me too, Billie,' I reminded her.

'Yes, but I'm shorter than everyone so it doesn't count.'

I laughed.

'I fucking love you, Billie O'Reilly.'

'I fucking love you, Clementine Ford.'

We grew a garden that summer, Billie and me. We planted seeds in fertile soil, and watered them daily. We lay in the hot sun and listened to fat, lazy bees drift from flower to flower—flowers that we coaxed into life and whose pollen would now give birth to more blooms. We listened to the sounds of the earth, grass tickling our cheeks as the rich scent of dirt twisted itself into the back of our throats. This was our time, and it was precious and perfect.

The garden has taken on a life of its own now, wild and free. It grows, even without us there to cultivate it. The time, like life, like love, like the beating of our own gloriously full hearts, goes on.

Every single moment of it.

LEAVE YOUR HUSBAND

I was a typical young girl in many ways. I enjoyed the literary works of Ann M. Martin and Francine Pascal. I had an extensive collection of stuffed animals, and I made sure to distribute their sleeping-in-the-bed rights evenly so as not to hurt any of their feelings. I liked twirling. And like most young girls raised on a diet of boyfriend stories and people-pleasing, I assumed that one day I would be married.

It wasn't a question of 'if' but of 'when'. Despite the limitless possibilities for adventure that childhood offered, 'settling down' seemed to be as much a natural outcome of adulthood as the cessation of pimples or knowing how to walk in heels. I wasted little energy worrying about the chap involved, presuming he would arrive just as the seasons did: indistinguishably at first, and then all of a sudden there. My husband would emerge into my life fully formed, the vagaries of courtship having been dealt with as if in a distant dream. One day I would be a young woman, finally allowed to wear lipstick; the next, I would be married.

That I had no particular desire for the ritual of marriage seemed irrelevant. I had never imagined my wedding day, nor spent lazy afternoons putting together composite profiles of men who would and wouldn't do. I'd never fake-married a boy (or girl) at school, nor attached a pillow case to my head and practised walking down a pretend aisle. My Barbie dolls (of which I had an extensive collection) did none of these things either, preferring instead to zip around in Barbie's Dream Car or spend vast quantities of time having sex with each other. A committed fan of movies like *Working Girl* and *Don't Tell Mom The Babysitter's Dead*, the visions I had of my future life more often than not involved me working as an ambitious secretary or conning my way into the inner circle of a fashion house and then bluffing my way out of a mess of my own making. There would be men, of course, but they would be a by-product of the real storyline of my life, which would feature adventure, independence and a fake identity, and not necessarily in that order. Still, the matter of a husband at some point seemed inevitable. This was simply what women *did*. Who was I to question how things worked?

As I entered adolescence and left the thrill of Barbie's sex life behind, I became more susceptible to the idea of The One and all that it entailed. Unfortunately, this coincided with the crushing insecurity of adolescence, a time in which I spent countless hours daydreaming about boys I believed would never, *could* never, want me. Standing behind the counter of the suburban Wendy's I worked at on the weekends, I'd concoct elaborate scenes in my head involving boys I liked, some of whom I knew from school and others whose tanned faces and perfect smiles graced the walls of my bedroom. In these fantasies, we never did much more than hold hands and kiss innocently, but the love we felt for each other was *real* and *intense* nonetheless.

At university, I graduated to pining for stormy-eyed boys whose truculent veneers I told myself concealed complex emotional depths and unexpectedly gentle fingers. I thought of these young men as enigmas to be solved, scattered pieces of a torn poem looking to be put back together, lost souls at risk of falling off the edge of the earth without the love of a good woman to save them—that woman being me, obviously. I imagined my beloved's face twisted into the tortured expression of a man who believes himself incapable of love because he is adrift in the Sea of Emptiness and cannot find his way back to shore. *But, but, but,* he would say, clasping my hands and pulling me to him, *you make me want to try.*

For a long time, I thought these fantasies marked me as a hopeless romantic, passionate and deep; my unwillingness to entertain the prospect of anything other than the most star-crossed of love affairs was clearly evidence of my own fantastically interesting emotional self. I longed for the day when one of these men would allow their walls to be broken down by me, and we could kiss to cement the merging of our souls. For love to be meaningful, surely it had also to be difficult in some way?

But with age comes wisdom, and eventually I realised the plain truth: that men who were skilled at being mean or sad were not secretly looking for women to save them. I had just watched *Reality Bites* too many times.

❣

After the torrid years of my twenties, with the series of broken hearts that decade brought (mostly mine, sometimes other people's), I met the man who would become my son's father.

We were at a music festival in regional Victoria. I was there by accident, having taken the ticket of my friend Valerie, a writer and editor I worked for who'd been called away at the last minute. A group of women from my roller derby league were going. I had been determined to become part of their inner circle since arriving in Melbourne less than six months earlier, and so I didn't let the fact I knew nothing about *listening* to music let alone *writing* about it stop me from agreeing to cover the festival in Valerie's place.

My friend Rosa arrived early to pick me up, and I stuffed my small bag into the boot of her already crammed acid green hatchback. I climbed into the front seat and tried to act as if this was the kind of thing I did all the time—packing bags in cool new cities and heading to music festivals to get drunk and not feel vaguely intimidated by all the drugs being passed around in front of me.

On the way, Rosa filled me in on the dynamics of the group we'd be camping with. Some of them I knew already from the two or three nights a week I spent being pummelled by them on rollerskates. Others were derby-adjacent at that point, having retired from the league before I'd arrived or being the partners of players past and present. As she talked, I tried to quell the feeling of nerves that was bubbling in my tummy. These women were *cool* and impressive, two things I was most avowedly not.

Rosa told me about the soon-to-be-ex-husband of one of them, an import from America who had come via New Zealand. He was a photographer, she said, and 'just absolutely one of the *sweetest* people you could ever meet'.

'Why did they break up?' I asked.

'Oh, there was nothing sinister,' she replied. 'Sometimes these things just happen.'

When we arrived, most of the group had already pitched their tents—one of them had even erected a small tent for me, for which I was extremely grateful (given the fact I hate anything to do with the practical elements of camping)—and they were gathered around a collection of eskies in the centre of the campsite, laughing.

As Rosa and I joined them, a man standing in the circle called out to her; this, she whispered, was the soon-to-be ex-husband she'd told me about. He was an inch or so taller than me and drinking from a beer can stuffed into a stubby holder. Some of the froth from it had caught on the edges of his moustache, which sat thick and lustrous on his upper lip. He was wearing a high-vis vest, and a lanyard printed with PHOTOGRAPHER hung around his neck. Rosa introduced us, and I reached out to shake his hand. He was nice-looking in the sense that he looked *nice*, but he was going through a marriage break-up, so I didn't consider the interaction much beyond that. After some polite small talk, I excused myself to put my bag in the tent.

I didn't talk to the American until later that afternoon, when he returned to the campsite from one of his shifts. I was too anxious to head to the actual music part of the festival, convinced people would be able to tell just by looking at me that I was far more au fait with Barbra Streisand than any of the bands on the festival program. It seemed safer to stay close to home base and, crucially, the goon bags of wine I had brought with me. Some of the other women and I were sitting around talking drunkenly about all the bad sex we'd had when he suddenly appeared, dropping the heavy camera bag he'd been hauling around and pulling up a chair.

Later, he would tell me he found the ribald nature of our conversation hilarious. As I would quickly discover, he isn't the kind of person to talk loudly about his sexual exploits, but he was amused by our enthusiasm for the topic, as many men are when they allow themselves to sit and listen quietly when women share the funny details of our lives.

As we all sat there trying to outdo each other with our terrible experiences of men, he interjected to say something so droll and dry that I collapsed immediately into a fit of giggles. Men who make me laugh have always been my particular weakness, and so it was that I fell, struck by Cupid's arrow.

Having been initially ambivalent to the soft-spoken man with the moustache, I spent the rest of the weekend keenly aware of his presence. I wanted to talk to him, but such was the force of my unexpected crush that I'd been struck mute. Instead, I watched him from a distance. *Pining.*

I'd been invited to appear as a panellist on a national current affairs show filmed in Sydney, so I had to leave the festival a day before it ended. Before I hopped on the train home, though, I caught one last set. It was golden hour, that time just before dusk when everything was bathed in an orange hue. First Aid Kit were playing, and he was taking photographs. I stood with our group and watched him, observing the way the late afternoon sun made his olive skin glow. My body buzzed as I watched this man, this unexpected delight, immersed in the creative practice of doing something he loved.

When the time came for me to leave, I hugged everybody goodbye and used the opportunity to pull him close and say it had been nice to meet him.

'You too!' he responded in his gentle American accent, a friendly smile on his face.

I gazed at the passing countryside as the train made its way back to Melbourne, thinking of the man and how I wanted to know him better. Before I lost my nerve, I opened up Facebook and searched for his name.

Add Friend, I tapped.

A few minutes later, I received a notification saying he had accepted.

❣

My plans to make the American fall in love with me were hindered slightly by the fact I was *technically* seeing someone at the time. We'd been set up by a mutual friend, who'd said the man in question was 'a huge fan'. I've since come to understand what a red flag this particular statement is, but I was young and foolish then, and considered this a compliment rather than a warning.

We had only been dating for two months, but I was already beginning to suspect he wasn't right for me. I noticed that I'd begun to tiptoe around his feelings, which seemed to have taken on an aggressive weight in recent weeks. He fancied himself as a writer of sorts, yet had failed to achieve the widespread literary success he'd perhaps expected. Consequently, he'd had to supplement the paltry income he earned from his writing by getting an office job. Shortly after we began dating, and just as my career was beginning to take off a bit, he had been made redundant. In a wild coincidence, his change in workplace status led to him discovering that all the things he had liked about me as a fan were the same things he hated about me as a lover.

Although he was enthusiastic about the upcoming television appearance, his behaviour pivoted sharply when I returned from Sydney. I was speaking at another event that night, a panel at the Malthouse Theatre in which an iconic Australian presenter would also be appearing. I'd invited him as my plus one, but he cancelled at the last minute, claiming to be tired.

Come over after, though, he texted, adding an x, a tiny gesture of intimacy that I had by then learned to grasp on to for reassurance.

When I was finished, I messaged to tell him I'd be along soon—I was just going to have a quick drink with the other panellists, including the iconic presenter.

Can you believe I'm sitting here with her, *of all people?!* I exclaimed.

Have fun, he replied. But there was no *x* this time.

Later, I rode my rickety old bike up to Northcote against a headwind, and pushed open the front door of his house, which he had left unlocked for me. He was coming out of the bedroom when I walked in, and one glance at his face should have been enough to make me turn around and ride home immediately. It was a look of pure disgust and hatred. To this day, I don't think anyone's ever looked at me like that, not even people who claim to truly despise me.

'Hey,' he spat, derision for me pouring out of him. He went into the bathroom and closed the door.

I tiptoed quietly into his bedroom, carefully removed my clothes and crawled beneath the blankets, full of shame for whatever it was I had done wrong. It must have been something egregious to offend him so badly, that much was clear, and I lay rigid on the very edge of the bed so as not to upset him even further. When he returned, it was with the same stony silence and simmering resentment. He climbed into bed next to me, turned his back and went to sleep without saying a word.

I slept fitfully, but when I woke the next morning he had a bright look on his face and gave me an enthusiastic hello.

'Hi!' I replied, confused but also pleased to be back in his good graces. 'You seem to be in a better mood this morning.'

'Ah, yeah.' He shrugged. 'Sorry about last night, I was just really tired.'

'It's okay,' I said, smiling at him.

But I had begun to feel that maybe it wasn't okay. That he was pressing a finger deep into my flesh, telling me to ignore the bruise that was already beginning to splinter out from it.

When I rode my bike home an hour or so later, I found myself thinking about the American man and the careful way he had held his camera. How he had looked as he'd cupped his hand around the screen and peered intently at the image he had captured, making sure he had done it justice.

❦

Over the next few days I scrolled through the American's Facebook page, searching for clues as to what kind of person he was. I knew he'd been 'in bands' while living in New Zealand, and I found evidence of this in his photo albums. Smoky, black-and-white pictures of him as a younger man, looking serious with a guitar strap slung over his broad shoulder. There were other images too, mostly of the festivals and gigs he'd covered.

He had a photographer's eye, that much was obvious. (Later, I would understand how much time and emotional energy he devoted to making each image 'perfect'.) Back then, though, my favourite photos were the ones of him laughing. He had a wide, genuine smile that seemed to be full of pure joy.

I hadn't yet broken up with the hack writer, but I found myself daydreaming about what it would be like to kiss the American in his stead.

I seized the opportunity to test the waters during the Melbourne International Comedy Festival. The American had posted about his dismay on discovering that Wanda Sykes's show had sold out, and I quickly sent Valerie an email.

Huge favour, I wrote. *Can I get a couple of tickets to review Wanda Sykes, please? No payment necessary, and I'll file the copy straight away!*

She approved the request quickly, and my heart skipped a beat. I opened a message box on the Facebook app and typed in the American's name.

Hey, I began. *I saw your post about Wanda Sykes. I actually have a couple of review tickets to see her show, and I haven't invited anyone yet. Do you want to come with me?*

He replied a few minutes later, enthusiastically accepting the invitation. My heart went from skipping beats to thudding wildly. I gave him the details and arranged to meet him for a drink before the show, then spent the next few days feeling sick with nerves that he would cancel, or worse, that he wouldn't.

But I needn't have worried. He turned up as planned, and we talked, laughed and drank until the wee hours of the morning, moving from the comedy venue to a whisky bar and then, finally, his living room. He had a cat, which caused my skin to break out in hives and my eyes to swell almost shut, but I persevered despite the risk of anaphylaxis. At some point, I confessed that I was seeing someone, which seemed to surprise him not because he thought we were on a date but because he had evidently assumed it wasn't one.

'I'm going to break up with him, though,' I told him, scratching my face manically. 'He's not a very nice person.'

I slept on his couch that night, and disappeared the next morning still covered in the telltale signs of *intense allergy to cats*. But we continued texting, and when I finally gave the hack writer the flick a week or so later, I wasted no time in asking the American to meet me for buttered rums at a pub in Melbourne's inner north.

So it was our love affair began and, with it, our life.

We'd been living together for three years when I informed him of my desire to have a child. I was thirty-four and had just signed a deal to write my first book. It seemed as if all the work I had put in during the gruelling slog of my late twenties and early thirties was finally paying off, so what better time to throw a wild bull into the proverbial china shop and add sleepless nights and a broken body to the mix?

Of course, I didn't know about the reality of newborns then. Nor was I prepared for how destructive those little creatures can be to relationships. The genteel life I imagined for myself was cast in soft, pastel focus. I would finally be a published author. I'd have a placid, chubby little baby who cooed at all the right times and cried only when absolutely necessary, which would be never. And I'd have a loving partner who supported me emotionally in both of these endeavours, understanding without question or conflict what needed to be done and simply getting on with it.

Things, as they say, didn't quite go according to plan.

My pregnancy was plagued by chronic anxiety, none of which was helped by the fact I was also on deadline for the book. He was absent for much of it, producing an album for a friend's band that was consuming all of his time and challenging his perfectionism. I felt like I had become the single stakeholder in a massive project we had started together, and the feeling only escalated once our son was born. The birth was traumatic, both physically and emotionally, and our adjustment to this new reality came as an even bigger shock. I resented the ease with which he seemed able to return to life as he knew it, as if nothing of consequence had really occurred. He resumed work on the album in the office downstairs, and I took care of the baby while diving straight back into writing, speaking and touring. I wrote articles and speeches in the documents folder on my phone, pushing the pram around for hours or strapping my son into a carrier and pounding the pavement. The days were long and lonely, and with a baby who wouldn't sleep unless connected directly to my body, they were also often suffocating. In the pre-dawn hours, after another night of broken sleep and relentless feeding, I'd look at the man lying asleep next to me, the one I'd fallen in love with over golden sunsets and buttered rums and think, *I hate you.*

One of the things I had always valued about our relationship was how independent we could be of each other—which is to say, I had valued how independent *I* could be. I was often travelling for work, sometimes announcing it at a moment's notice. I was still playing roller derby, a sport that required a lot of time out for training and an almost equal amount of time for socialising. I am an introvert by nature, and the emotional toll of being so busy also means I have to recharge in solitude. When it was just the two of us, it was an ideal situation. But the introduction of a third, defenceless creature to our situation upended all of this. For the first time in my life, I needed help. I needed respite. I needed to feel supported in some fairly basic ways. And like so many women stunned by the reality of the 'happy ever after', I felt myself to be abandoned.

I experienced the shock of motherhood and its impact on our relationship as a huge betrayal, and I blamed him for most of it. My book, a feminist manifesto and memoir, had been released when our son was seven weeks old. I had a public reputation for being a 'man-hater' whose feminist wrath had made her the scourge of trolls everywhere. For years, I'd been telling women not to tolerate sexism from men. How could someone like *me* have been caught in the terrible trap of domestic drudgery, while a man skated alongside her with very little disruption to his life or any awareness of the labour that went into facilitating it?

I wasn't just angry and hurt about the new reality of my life. I was *embarrassed*.

But I was also in the grip of the early childhood years, when it takes all of your energy just to keep treading water. So I persevered, trying to keep us all afloat even though it seemed I was carrying the world on my shoulders. And it took so much out of me that, in the end, I had no energy left to keep from drifting away on the current until he became nothing but a speck in the distance.

❣

When the first blossoms of love were beginning to open between us, I asked the American how he could be ready for a relationship so soon after the end of his previous one. He and his ex-wife had been together for fourteen years, moved continents together, become adults together. That was a lot of history to compete with.

He said something that has stayed with me, all these years later.

'When you break up after that long, you've been breaking up for a long time.'

This is true for so many people, and in the end it was also true for us. People hold on to the fragments long after they're able to be put back together, wanting through sheer will to evade what they already know can't be reversed. Sometimes things are just over, and no amount of hoping for that to be untrue can make it so. We had been breaking up for a long time when I finally said the words out loud to him, but the moment I did I was flooded with relief. I took no pleasure in hurting him, but I had been hurting myself. My desires were modest, but they were important. I wanted to stop feeling sad. I wanted to start feeling happy.

In the months before I decided to leave my relationship, I found myself thinking about what I wanted my life to look like. Did I want to wake up at fifty and realise that I had no idea who I even was anymore beyond being someone's mother or someone's wife? We had never been married, but nor did it feel right in the end to think of us as partners. Partnership is a commitment. We must consciously choose to be someone's partner every day. To have curiosity about their lives. To support their goals and dreams, and to make them feel seen.

I didn't feel seen, and the knowledge left me with a deep wound. Outside of my home, I was championed and celebrated. My work made a difference to the lives of girls and women, and because of this I felt confident to use my voice to speak up against injustice. I was achieving a level of notoriety in my career that was both flattering and professionally fulfilling. Yet despite this, when I laid my head down at night I felt invisible. I spent so much of my life taking care of other people, from my son and his father to my friends and the women who wrote to me to share the crushing details of their own lives.

Who was taking care of *me*?

I didn't want to spend my life receding into the walls the way so many women have been condemned to throughout history.

I couldn't understand why this man who claimed to love me didn't also seem to notice that I was disappearing.

As the discord between us grew and my temper flared more frequently, I had a vision of our son in the future. I pictured him as a teenager, telling a friend or a lover how much he hated his parents. How he never wanted to be as miserable as them, as soulless, as deprived of love and passion. I imagined him older than that still, a young man who looked at us with a mixture of pity and disdain. Who would say to friends at dinner parties, *I don't think my parents have had sex in years*, while they all laughed in horror, convinced such a fate could never befall them.

Ultimately, this was perhaps what motivated me most of all. I wanted my son to see in his mother a woman who was happy. A woman who grasped life with both hands and who wasn't afraid to take a leap into the unknown. I wanted him to understand that women deserve to be seen, and I wanted him to see *me* as a multidimensional person with dreams and desires that existed well beyond picking up after someone else. I have always wanted the best for him—to have friends, to be kind, to have food to eat, to know that his dreams matter. Why hadn't I included a happy mother in my vision of what a *good life* meant for him?

Sometimes love means having the courage to end what is no longer working. Love for other people. Love for ourselves.

❣

On an afternoon in late May, on a day so warm it didn't seem possible that winter lurked just around the corner, a day that saw hordes of inner northerners flock to neighbourhood parks and gardens to laugh and drink and flirt and feel all the light-hearted promises that life has to offer, as the noise from the passing trains nearby marked the steady passing of time, I piled the last of my things into my car and drove away from the house I had shared with a man I had once loved.

I did not cry as I drove away, just as I had not cried when I peeled the photo magnets I'd ordered during our earlier, pre-child life from the fridge and tossed them into the bin. I had not cried as I emptied my clothes from drawers and cupboards—the cupboard he had insisted be called a closet because it didn't store cups in it. It was a joke I had once laughed at, until it stopped being funny, the way so many things do when love walks out and bitterness takes its place. I felt nothing as I packed a suitcase and zipped the lid closed. There were no tears as I steadfastly and routinely determined what it was I needed and what I was happy to be rid of in this, the simultaneous downsizing and upsizing of my life.

I had not cried as I listened to him ask me again, *Why? Why are you doing this?* Nor had I cried as he implored me to think about our son, whom I had apparently not thought about at all when I broke up with him on our couch: the couch that I had shopped for and bought and then assembled in our previous flat, which I had found to rent and moved us into and to which we had brought our son on the second night of his life. The same couch that I had disassembled myself and moved into the house I had found and rented for us all nine months later, because it had a garden and a porch and a second bathroom that would belong only to me, which I told myself would maybe sort of perhaps possibly make up for the fact that in this house, this three-bedroom house that I had found, the only space I could reasonably let myself have *just for me* was that second bathroom, because the first bedroom was where we both slept on the bed I had bought and put together myself when I was six months pregnant, and the second bedroom was where I set up our son's cot, spending frustrated, heart-bruising nights alone trying to teach him how to sleep before retreating to sit on that couch, with its ever-growing web of stains and crumbs, and drink large glasses of wine and listen to tears, the baby's yes but mine also—the tears that I would later be accused of being too cold to produce. The second bathroom could be my space, because it just seemed to be accepted as pre-ordained that the third bedroom would belong to him and his computer and papers and mementoes and recording equipment and mess that never saw the sunlight. At the very least, I insisted that his clothes be stored in the cupboard—sorry, closet—in the spare room—sorry, *his* room—so that I didn't have to step around them in the bedroom that was not mine but ours.

I did not cry as I sat on the couch that night and said calmly and with what I hoped was a kind spirit, 'I think we should break up.'

'Is there someone else?' he asked, reaching for whatever might make the situation feel better, because it's always been better for the reason to be someone else than for the reason to just *be*.

'No,' I replied. 'It's not about that.'

He cried. I didn't.

My refusal to cry was a flaw of mine apparently, an indicator of the lack of feeling I had brought not only to the split but also to the months of polite small talk and occasional blow-ups which marked that tremulous period of cohabitation between break-up and breakout.

'You never cry!' he would exclaim, exasperated with me. 'What's wrong with you? Don't you feel anything?!'

It was true. I hadn't cried much over the break-up, save for a few mournful tears here and there for what might have been, what could have been preserved, *if if if.* But by then my heart had sealed over, retreated from the sun and its warmth even as spring and summer had unfurled around us. I had watched myself moving slowly out of the relationship long before I moved out of the house, but he, like so many people seemingly blindsided by the end, had not noticed.

And so I drove away that day, away from the couch and the bed and the whitegoods that I had found and bought for the house that I had also found, with its garden and porch and second bathroom (mine) and its cupboards (or closets, depending on how you view things).

It was past mandarin season, but they hung there heavy anyway on the fruit trees that lined the garden. I told our neighbours to help themselves, and I left them behind too.

I drove to my new flat, a flat that I had found myself but this time just for me, and stood on its balcony. The train line stretched alongside me to the left, the frequent dings of the crossings more or less letting me know what time it was. No matter where you find yourself, time marches forward regardless. I watched as passengers stepped into its carriages, people moving about the world with lives and problems and desires and secrets and hopes and dreams and fears just like mine, just as valid and real as I had decided mine were. Inside, my son sat playing with his toys on the plush rug, the rug that I had found and bought and laid out on the floorboards in the living room: my floorboards, my living room, where if shoes were ever kicked off carelessly and left in the middle of the floor it would be okay, because they would be my shoes and it would be my floor—a reminder of my messiness, yes, but not my sadness. I would never look at my own shoes discarded on my floor in the middle of my living room, in my flat, and feel despair.

I looked at the new home that I had made and I wondered at all the possibilities left to me. Some of them would be mundane, but others would be thrilling. There would be love, I knew that. There would be laughter. There would be magic. My heart would slowly heal, and the cuts, the beautiful cuts that remained, would leave space now to let new light in.

There's a dish I often made while living at the old house. One of the central ingredients is mushrooms, but I had always left them out because the man I lived with didn't like mushrooms. I had tried so hard, as we all do, as even he did, to take care with the tiny details. To smooth the path for the people I love to try to make their lives a little bit easier.

'How do you like the food?' I would sometimes ask him, hating myself for wanting praise and gratitude for something so minor as a meal.

'It's good,' he would reply, putting a forkful in his mouth. 'I'll only ever let you know if something's bad.'

Shortly after moving into my new flat, I sat down to eat that same dish. Outside, it was cold and dark. *June.* As was my habit, I had left the mushrooms out, and I didn't realise it until halfway through the meal.

Next time, I thought to myself, *I'll add the mushrooms. I can do that now*, I thought. *That is a thing that I can do.*

❣

I love living alone.

I love having my own space. I love that the things in my house are my things, that the mess is my mess. I love that the clothes that sometimes find their way onto the floor are my clothes, and that the only person responsible for picking them up is me. I love that I can come and go as I please on the days of the week when my son is with his father. I love that the time I have with my son now is untainted by domestic resentments and exhaustion. I love that I can bring people home with me or not, have sex with them or not, fall in love over and over again—and that I will never be in service to a man again.

I wonder if I have always been meant to live this way and simply lacked the role models to show that it was possible. I should have taken my childhood ambivalence towards marriage and investigated it further. Alice and I often discuss what we want from future relationships, and I find myself flabbergasted whenever she says she can see herself living with someone again.

'But how?!' I ask, unable to conceal my incredulity, at which she always laughs.

I imagine a world in which our entire notion of 'family' is reinvented. Where women's desire for motherhood is divested from our belief that it can only happen if we enter into a nuclear partnership. I feel as if I have the best of both worlds now. I am a mother, and this brings to my life a particular meaning and resonance that is important to me. But I am also a woman outside of this, and I don't need to struggle to remember this fact. I move easily between the two states of being, without the risk of one consuming the other.

There is something else too: the knowledge that what seemed to be destroyed beyond all repair can be nudged back into wild life.

From the ruins of our relationship, the American and I have emerged stronger and more able to see the evidence of what our love was capable of: the son we made together, and whose discovery of the world reminds us of why it all mattered so much. I love the time the three of us spend together as a family. I love watching how the relationship of father and son has bloomed since I extracted myself from the centre of it. The tenderness with which the American man parents the small boy, the ways in which he has stepped so fully into the role of caregiver, teacher, guide and protector. I don't know that this would have been possible had I not forced a situation in which it was unavoidable.

We eat together frequently, going to our local pub for cheeseburgers and pinball. This is where the man and I have the kind of conversations we used to have, our son drawing next to us or running around the beer garden with other children. On other days, we might take him to the park. We've started having movie nights, showing him the classics of our own childhood or discovering new ones together. We've been on holidays together, birthdays and public holidays spent in cabins or caravans. Our son is still young enough that he likes to sleep with us, and on these weekends we all crawl into bed together, him nestled between us. We're a family—and even though what that means has changed in some fundamental ways, the fact that we are a family will always be the same.

It took a long time to get to this point. In the early days of our separation, when I was still angry enough to be inconvenienced by having to deal with the practicalities of it, we could hardly speak to each other without fighting. We did handover for our son quickly, with no conversation beyond what was absolutely necessary regarding his care. We had many a bitter phone call that ended with me hanging up on him, refusing to give a single inch on my position or to give any credence to his feelings.

I had felt myself so oppressed by the intensity of domestic life and cohabitation that it seemed I was drowning in it. When

I left, I pulled back so far that he and everything he had meant to me became almost invisible.

But time is a great healer of wounds, particularly when one makes the decision to treat them with care. Now, I feel as if we have all moved back into focus. Where we have ended up doesn't look exactly the same as where we began. There are some things missing that will be gone forever. But we have gained a lot too: aspects of love that would never have been possible had we not redefined what we were and what we could be to each other. Just as I needed to leave in order to find that focus, he needed me to go so that he could once again see who I was. I have peeled myself from the wall, and I stand here in full form. I am known. And I find that the love I once had, that struck me in a golden field on a late afternoon, has returned in some form. It will never be what it was, but it is also richer and more promising in so many other ways now that both it and I are allowed to run wild.

Years ago, the man and I set out on a voyage together, full of optimism about where we were headed. But we ran into a storm and could not navigate our way through. Our boat dashed against the rocks, and we washed up on different parts of an unknown shore, bruised and battered. We built shelters there, adding to them as time went on, each of our lives extending beyond the thing that had brought us there in the first place. We added rooms to our shelters, decorations and trinkets and happy memories of our time in this new land, this new way of being.

And eventually, the edges of those shelters met.

We wave to each other now from our makeshift stoops. We pass things back and forth over the fence. Stories. Wine. Food. Laughter. Our son. Sometimes, we sit on the shore together and watch the sunset, marvelling at how we made something beautiful out of so much wreckage. We might talk for hours, the stars scattering across the sky one by one, until fatigue sets in and we are called to our own beds in our own shelters in the new but different life we have made together.

We will live like this forever, I think. He's family, and always will be. I have chosen well.

❦

There is a city you have heard of. A place to start again. You want to go there, but you're scared. I understand.

Be brave.

They say it takes roughly two years to settle into a new city. Learning the rhythms of that new place, making new friends, finding the best places to eat and where to stroll on a Sunday in order to feel all the possibilities of the world.

For some people, being single is like leaving behind everything they've known and starting again somewhere new. If you've never experienced the joy of that land, it might take some time to adjust. There will be days where you feel homesick for what you've known, even if you had good reasons for leaving. There will be nights when you might cry, feeling the weight of what lies ahead of you. Learning to navigate a new city and all its secrets can be overwhelming, and there will be days when you feel like you made a mistake.

But slowly, the city will open itself up to you. You'll make new friends, arrange to meet them in bars and restaurants that are becoming fast favourites. You'll laugh and you'll cry, but about things that are happening now and not things that happened back then, in that place you left.

You'll wake up early and sit in the stillness of the morning light, sipping coffee made by people who know your name and how you like it. You'll walk through streets and notice houses with interesting details that touch your heart, and listen to music that reminds you of a park you sat in last week. You'll date people in the city, and some of them will feel more exciting than others but none of them will feel essential to your happiness, which is richer now and more robust than it was before, when you thought the only way to have it was to give half of it away.

You will do all of these things until the city is no longer big and unfamiliar and lonely and terrifying but has suddenly, inexplicably and unexpectedly become your home.

And one day, you will take a newly arrived resident out and you will show them all the things about the city that are wonderful. You will show them the things that saved you when you were scared and lonely. You'll take them to the top of a hill to show them how the city looks at the exact time the sun hits it in late afternoon, and you'll tell them where to find the best coffee and which real estate agents to avoid. You will show them what life can look like. What it *will* look like.

This is your city now. This is your home.

Welcome home.

6

BAD TEXTER

I met the Bad Texter for the first time on a cold night in June. I'd come across his profile on one of the many dating apps that flood the market now, turning romance and all its many possibilities into a sad smorgasbord of half-picked-at food and wilted lettuce leaves. I'd swiped past it a few times, but it kept being refreshed into my feed. He was younger than me by a handful of years but still in the same ballpark, so I didn't think it too odd to keep looking. There was something about one of his answers that made me laugh each time I saw it and when I was still laughing the third or fourth time, I decided to send him a message.

That's a handsome dog, I wrote, referring to a photograph he had of his pet pooch. *I like his proud ears.*

Thank you, he replied. He told me the dog's name, which I promptly forgot and needed to be corrected on later.

We chatted back and forth, and decided that we liked each other well enough to arrange to meet for a drink.

I had suggested we meet at a bar on the corner of my street, but he texted as I was leaving my flat to say it was closed.

Wait there, I replied. *I'm coming and there's somewhere else we can go.*

I had almost cancelled the date that night, a common habit in the lawless land of internet dating. Everyone is racked by anxiety, too afraid to meet and be faced with disappointment or, worse, see disappointment in someone else's eyes.

I'm not here for a penpal! so many of the profiles claim, and yet it turns out that this is exactly what a lot of people want. Someone to whom they can construct a personality and pose in front of, dipping in and out as they please, circling numerous conversations at once, recycling jokes and memes and come-ons stolen from other people before ultimately going to bed alone at night, safe in the knowledge they haven't given away anything about themselves. I'm as guilty of it as anyone. Texting I can do. Living is a little harder.

Still, I resisted the urge to feign sickness that night and pulled together an outfit. This was when my hair was cropped short, and I pushed the fringe into a quiff on my head, carefully winged my eyes with liquid black eyeliner and added a slash of bright red lipstick.

I'm going on a date, I texted to a boy I'd been having a secret flirtation with, sending him a photograph, one of about seven that I'd taken in the attempt to appear effortlessly attractive. *How do I look?*

Ravishing, he responded.

The compliment put a spring in my step as I exited the apartment building to meet the other man in question.

I had only been separated from my son's father for a few months, but had been on something of a whirlwind tour of inner-north bachelors. There was the skateboarder, who drank whisky with me in bed. The English teacher, who halted proceedings one night to ask me if I'd just invited him over for sex and if I even liked him (spoken answer: 'Yes, of course!'; real answer: 'Define "like"?'). The economist, whose stance on splitting bills ('I never pay for anyone else and I never expect anyone to pay for me') put me off, even though it was technically fair enough—I slept with him anyway, and found that while he was evidently a Scrooge when it came to dinner, he was exceptionally selfless in regard to dessert. The bartender, who I hated but not as much as I hated myself for being attracted to him. The photographer, with whom I had one of the best first dates of my life, kissed twice, but who instead of my lover became one of my very best friends. And, finally, the man with the completely hairless crotch who I drunkenly unloaded my postpartum insecurities onto while having sex and then understandably never heard from again.

I have since become far more circumspect about the people I date and go to bed with (mostly none), but the time post separation is a giddy carnival, with countless sideshows to see and enjoy. You don't always land the ball in the clown's mouth, but your appetite for the game is still fresh.

And so I headed out on that cold Monday night, expecting little but open to anything. Just before I rounded the corner, I paused to pull out my phone and open the camera. I fixed my hair, checked my lipstick. All seemed well.

In my memory, he was wearing a baseball cap when I first saw him, but I think in reality it was a beanie. What I mean to say by that is that everything in this story is true, in one way or another.

❣

'Hello!' I said to him, in what I hoped was a jovial and inviting manner.

'Hello,' he said, his lips curving into a smile. 'It's closed!' he repeated. 'How rude of them!'

'Terribly rude,' I agreed, smiling back. I was relieved to see he wasn't too different from his photographs, which is a more common problem than you'd think—yet another reason people are so often reluctant to meet.

'We can go to the pretend dive bar down the street,' I said. 'It has wine and beer, but lower your expectations for the quality of both.'

He looked past me to the kebab shop on the other corner.

'I just want to go over there and see what a "momo" is first,' he told me. 'Do you know what it is?'

'I've no idea,' I said, falling into step beside him as we crossed the street towards the flashing neon sign, trying not to let the natural awkwardness of the first five to ten minutes of a date overwhelm me.

I listened as he asked the kebab guy what a momo was and then decided that no, he didn't want one after all, and we walked back out to the street.

'Right!' he said. 'Let's go!'

We exchanged the usual nervous chitchat on the way, neither of us yet having a drink behind which to hide our insecurities. I asked something specific about his job and joked about the kinds of people he was forced to work alongside every day. He was a good conversationalist, batting the ball back and forth with me and seemingly comfortable with making fun of himself. By the time we reached the bar, the tension had eased enough for me to think we would have a good time, and I wouldn't instead spend the next thirty minutes wondering how long I needed to stay before I could politely make my excuses, return home and watch old episodes of *Gavin and Stacey* in my underwear.

By the end of the first drink, I had decided I liked him. And because I liked him, I began to feel self-conscious about the way my lips pulled up over my gums whenever I laughed too hard, which I was doing a lot of. After the next drink, I told him the long and complicated story of my father's second marriage, and he produced the required gasps and exclamations of shock that I felt the tale warranted. By the end of the third drink I was inviting him back to my house for a fourth drink, and sometime halfway into the fifth, after he had turned to me and asked, 'Can I kiss you?', I invited him to come to bed.

Afterwards, when I was drifting into a dream, I opened my eyes for a moment and saw that he was looking at me. He smiled, and the warmth of it wrapped around my body like a blanket. I smiled back, and we fell asleep face to face, arms nearly touching.

He left obscenely early the next morning, having arranged to meet a friend for a game of squash. I would learn later that this was the kind of thing he did; not leaving early, I mean, although he did that too, but playing squash. Who plays squash these days? He did, and the fact of it endeared him to me more.

It was still dark outside when he kissed me goodbye.

'Thanks for a great date,' he said. 'Now go back to sleep!'

I waved goodbye, but as soon as I heard the front door close I picked up my phone and opened the app we had been chatting on.

You're sensational, I wrote. *My number's 04———. Text me.*

He texted not long after. *No, YOU'RE sensational. Let's go out again.*

A train pulled into the station outside my window, bringing passengers home from night shifts and picking up new ones to take to work.

I would love that, I replied, then switched my phone off and went back to sleep.

❦

When I woke up for the second time that morning, I took my computer to my local cafe, ordered a coffee and set to group texting my inner circle about the 'superb date' I'd had the night before. They grilled me on the essentials, all of which I was extremely complimentary about. The important thing, I said, was that he had made me laugh and I liked him.

Will you see him again? my friend Nathan asked.

I hope so! I replied. *I'm not going to organise it though.*

While poring through the rubble of my long-term relationship, I had determined never again to fall into the pattern of being the 'planner'. Of activities, of holidays, of presents, of an entire life together. Acts of service being one of my love languages, I had done these things in the beginning as a way of showing my devotion. *Look at all these ways I can take care of you!* I had tried to say, not realising the message that would eventually be received: *I don't need you to take care of me.*

It had been so long since I'd had someone plan something with my needs in mind that I was surprised—blown away even—when I received a text message from him a few days later suggesting not only that we see each other the following Monday, but including a list of possible activities for me to choose from: active (bouldering or bowling), cerebral (arthouse movie), trashy (Netflix), or fancy (wine and cheese on Lygon Street).

The thought of bouldering didn't appeal—I hadn't liked him long enough to let him see me with a sweaty face—so I suggested we do the movie and the cheese.

He sent me a few options from the cinema's website, some of which I was pleased to discover included women in them, which I had learned was not always guaranteed when it came to men's tastes.

I'm excited, he wrote.

Are you excited about poring through the movie listings or about our date? I asked.

Our date! he replied. *I could drop everything and see a movie right now if I wanted to. YOU are the *secret ingredient*.*

My stomach did a little flip, and I blushed.

I'm excited to sit in a dark movie theatre and make out with you, I texted back after a minute or two. *I like-like you.*

Perhaps this was too eager of me, but I had been out of the dating game for a long time. More to the point, the last time I was *in* the dating game was before the confidence-boosting years of my thirties. I had lived with a man, gone through the terrible anxiety of pregnancy and the trauma of birth, survived the newborn years and a relationship breakdown. I wasn't interested in being coy or insecure about my feelings, and I assumed (incorrectly, as subsequent years of internet dating have taught me) that men would respond positively to such forthrightness. Misjudging men's appreciation of things—clever girls, forthright girls, funny girls—has evidently always been a special skill of mine. But I liked him and, as I had not yet been crushed by this state of modern romance and made cynical in regard to its purpose, I saw no harm in telling him how I felt.

We arranged to meet the following Monday, but when I woke up that morning I instinctively knew it wasn't going to happen. I say instinctively, but maybe this is just what we always say when our suspicions are confirmed.

I knew it.

I just had a feeling about it.

Don't ask me how I knew, I just did.

Either way, I expected at some point to receive a cancellation message. *I'm so sorry*, it would say. *Something's come up.* Or, *Could we reschedule? I'm not feeling well.*

I had sent messages like this myself and knew the protocol well. It isn't necessarily that you don't like the person or enjoy their company; it's that you don't trust your memory of those things, and worry that it might have all been a fluke. What if flirtations that had felt easy and natural last time were clunky and awkward the second time around? Or, worse, what if you actually really liked them but *they* decided that you weren't as great on a second viewing?

I was sitting at my desk when my phone dinged shortly after 9 am.

Hey, it said. *I'm really sorry to do this, but could we reschedule? I think I'm getting sick! I would rather come and be in good form than be petulant, which I think I will be if I go out tonight.*

Although I'd anticipated it, deep down I was really hoping to be proven wrong. So when it happened as expected, I felt both resigned and stupidly disappointed.

Of course! I replied, excessive enthusiasm being one of my finely tuned defence mechanisms. *That's absolutely fine. We'll see each other sometime I'm sure. I hope you feel better!*

I waited for the two green ticks to appear on the screen to indicate he'd read my message, but they stayed grey.

In fact, the message stayed unchecked for the rest of the day, which had the very welcome effect of turning my disappointment into irritation. Cancelling on a date was one thing—we've all done that—but it was just *rude* to do it and then not even wait to see if the person in question knew or would be turning up later that night with a carefully selected outfit and an architecturally sound bouffant. I decided he was a flake after all, deleted his number from my phone and set about forgetting him entirely.

But a week or so later, he showed up again, texting me to see how I was. The tone was familiar and friendly, and it didn't take me long to figure out it was him even though I'd deleted him from my contacts. I was still vaguely irritated by the manner in which he'd cancelled our date, but I'd distanced myself sufficiently from both the situation and him to not care all that much, a fact that I'm sure made me more attractive because nothing arouses our desire more than someone who makes it clear they have zero fucks to give.

He invited me to drop by a friend's house that Saturday night and I said I would try, but when the time came I was busy snorting coke in a bathroom in Fitzroy and told him as much over text.

I've just snorted a line of coke off the back of my phone, I wrote, *so I think I may be indisposed for the next few hours. Perhaps later?*

On reflection, this was the moment in which my control over the situation peaked and I had the most power. I was the cool one, out wearing disco pants in a scungy bar in Fitzroy and taking *drugs* with a devil-may-care attitude. I was what Alice calls 'a scarce resource'. I could take him or leave him, and was happy on this occasion to choose the latter. He was just some dude, after all. Who cares about that? Women were coming up to me and telling me how much they loved my work! How they were so excited to meet me! How I had changed their lives!

I was l u m i n e s c e n t. I was inviting. I was delightful. I was high as a kite on fucking drugs and I was the life of the party! *I can't come meet you, man, I'm communing with the universe! Also, I'm super fucking off my chops!*

Oh, how the tables turn.

Over the next few weeks and months, there would rarely be a time when I wouldn't have dropped *everything* to see him, never letting him know how fastidiously I had worked to reschedule my life in order to appear effortlessly, seamlessly available.

I cringe at the thought now, of course. But what are we to do when love—or a beast that looks an awful lot like it—has us in the unforgiving grip of its jaws?

But all that angst is yet to come. For now, we are in Fitzroy, aloof and free.

Would you still like to go on that second date? he asked me a few days later.

Mmmm, I replied. *I would. But I'm worried we might have missed the window.*

Well, we'll never know unless we try! he responded.

That's true! I conceded. *Okay. Let's do it.*

I think sometimes about what might have happened had I said no. The months of emotional agony I might have saved myself, brought on entirely by my own romantic notions and refusal to accept the lessons I'd been taught almost two decades earlier by some of the most influential figures in early twenty-first-century history: that four is the perfect number for brunch, your friends are the loves of your life and, sometimes, he's just not that into you.

❣

Thwarted love affairs can taint the most inconsequential things, and as it happens I can no longer pass the kebab shop on the corner of my street without feeling a tiny pang of, well, not quite *longing*, but something like it. And I have never been able to rewatch the superbly witty film *Booksmart*, with all of its clever observations about feminism, intelligence, sexuality and friendship, because this is the movie the Bad Texter and I went to see on our second, perfect date, and now when I think of blue boilersuits and berets, I think of sitting in the dark and whispering, 'I wish this movie was terrible so I could just make out with you instead.' But it wasn't terrible, and we watched and laughed and made quiet comments to each other, and afterwards we had cheese and wine and talked about the demise of our previous relationships. So low is the bar women set for men that I remember being impressed and *grateful* when he pulled out his credit card to pay at the end, and made a point to tell him how unused to that kind of behaviour I was, having paid for most things not just in my previous relationship but in fact in almost all of my relationships with men.

'Oh!' he replied, smiling. 'Well, that just makes me want to do it more!'

He held my hand as he walked me to my car, and we kissed in the middle of Faraday Street.

'When can we do this again?' he asked.

I told him the nights of the week I was free, lightly reminding him that I had a child.

'Yes, of course,' he said. 'Well, let's organise something.'

I kissed him again and climbed into my car, wrestling with that familiar, terrible feeling so many of us have—that to be a mother is a liberation in so many ways but also a constraint. As I turned the engine over, I imagined a life for myself that was unburdened and free; a life in which I could go out any night of the week and behave as if I were twenty-five again, but with the confidence that comes from being thirty-eight years old and able to afford nice sheets. I could appreciate what it meant to be single and untethered, both in the solitude it would bring and the opportunity for romantic escapades unimpeded by the responsibility of dinner, bath and bedtime rituals. I let myself think of it fiercely for the ten to fifteen minutes it took to get home, and then I went inside, paid the babysitter, took my make-up off and climbed into bed next to my son and whispered, 'I love you I love you I love you,' terrified that my brief moment of wishing for something else would result in the Goblin King coming and taking him away, just as I had asked him to do so many times before.

❣

A week or so later, we met at a small wine bar in North Fitzroy. It was the kind of place that works so hard to be unpretentious it can't help but be slightly pretentious in the process, but I liked how dimly lit it was and also, if truth be told, I'm quite pretentious myself. I was waiting for him at the bar, poured into a black and white striped bodysuit and carefully angled in what I imagined was a winsome pose, when I felt his hand gently press against my back.

'Hello!' he said, leaning down to kiss me. As his lips pressed against mine, I heard knives clattering on plates, glasses clinking and a low thrum of chatter. The world remains in motion, even when the most extraordinary things are happening within it.

We spent the next few hours drinking wine and chatting animatedly about politics, relationships and which memes we felt best relayed humanity's deepest flaws. In the dim light of the bar, I listened as he told me about his ex-girlfriend; they had broken up once, got back together, and then broke up a second time. When he said that she hated how sporadic his communication was, I resisted the urge to admit I could understand her frustration. I was in constant dialogue with my friends throughout the day, across numerous different platforms, sometimes talking to one person on two or three mediums at the same time. Anything less than incessant chatter felt to me like an act of borderline hostility.

'Why did you want to try again?' I asked him, enjoying the relaxed access I was being given to his intimate thoughts and feelings.

'Oh, because she's an amazing person!' he replied, an answer I enjoyed significantly less.

We talked about how precious things between people can be broken, and how sometimes it's impossible to repair the damage no matter how carefully we try. I told him about my first great love, whom I had been able to forgive for abandoning me during two abortions but to whom I could not extend the same compassion when he cheated on me two weeks after my mother died. He told me about his first great love, who had been older than him by a few years and who had broken his heart. I listened, nodding sympathetically, resisting the urge to ask all the things I suddenly longed to know.

What did she look like?

Was she funny?

Are you still in love with her, in some way?

At some point, I was overcome with the urge to touch him and so I put my hand on his knee and asked if that was okay. He brushed salt from his fingers and grabbed my hand with both of his in response, holding it there gently as we kept talking about other things.

During our conversation, a woman I knew walked past with her own date. We said hello and exchanged pleasantries, and I introduced her to him. I enjoyed the way the words fell out of my mouth, my hand sweeping across to catch them as I gestured in his direction. *This is* _____.

As I watched them chat briefly, I gave myself permission to think that there might be more of these kinds of introductions. Some of them would be planned and some of them would be spontaneous, but they would unfold around me steadily until there was no one left for him to meet. He and I would become a *we* and an *us*, included together in invitations and enquired after if one of us couldn't make it. This was what merging lives looked like—and although I hadn't asked for this or even been looking for it, I realised I would welcome it for *this* life, *this* man. Wasn't this how love arrived? Without notice or warning, but never without reason?

Afterwards, I walked him home and we kissed on his bed until my Uber arrived. It was a spectacular kiss, slow enough to be tender but electric enough to cause the hairs on my arms to stand up and a furnace to roar to life deep in the pit of my belly. I cursed the fact we both had to work the next day, because I felt sure that had he removed the weight of my clothes then and there I might have ascended to a higher plane of existence.

His hound, the one with the proud ears, was nestled between us and he broke the tension by asking if I'd ever made out with someone while leaning over a dog before.

'I haven't,' I replied, 'but I never shy away from new experiences.'

It was a drizzly night, characteristic of Melbourne in July, and he stood at the door as I left through the creaky gate.

'Text me when you get home,' he said.

'I will,' I replied, smiling. And then I was gone, in both senses of the word.

❦

We continued on in this way for a few weeks, seeing each other when we could and texting about this, that and the other. I could still be sent into a tizzy by the unpredictable nature of the contact, but I hadn't yet reached a state of frenzied angst about it.

About eight weeks or so into our courtship, he invited me to a movie trivia night with some of his friends. It had been years since I'd been in the dating game, but I remembered 'meeting the friends' as being one of those things with its own delicate set of rules. You can casually meet friends on a second or third date and it means nothing, the friends being just as unfamiliar and unknown to you as the person you're interested in exploring further. But meeting friends after a sustained period of dating, when limbs have been entangled, secrets have been confessed and lips have been kissed many times over . . . well, this is a different thing altogether. It's an invitation to be screened, assessed for suitability and then (hopefully) included in a life. When you invite someone to meet your friends, you're asking if they'd like to be *known* to the people you love most.

I wanted so much to be known, and so I accepted with both enthusiasm and terror. I took care with my outfit, wrapping my head in a scarf to cover the too-short haircut I had succumbed to after a recent weekend in Sydney, insecure about how unfeminine it made me feel (which was a few steps below the already baseline level of unfeminine I felt on an ongoing basis). He had come straight from work and was wearing a suit, a fact that amused me but also stirred a generosity of feeling, because men in suits always seem to me like little boys playing dress-ups.

I tried my best to charm and delight the people who—magically, it seemed!—were allowed to orbit freely around this human of exceptional qualities without fear of being considered too enthusiastic or uncool. I had answers for questions pertaining to the most mainstream of the movies referenced (this being one of my particular areas of expertise) and I basked in the warm glow of thinking I had performed well. I was conscious of appearing relaxed and low key, but when he reached for my hand under the table I curled my fingers around his and hoped no one would hear the sound of my heart beating thunderously against my chest. When it came time to say goodbye to everyone, it was with hugs and an expressed desire to repeat the experience.

A successful audition, I thought.

Afterwards, he and I walked to a nearby wine bar and flirted in the candlelight. I told him about an essay I'd read in *The Paris Review*, the one everyone was reading at the time about the woman who leaves her fiancé a week before their wedding and joins a scientific research expedition to follow the migration of whooping cranes. In the piece, the writer C.J. Hauser describes how deeply she buried her needs in a relationship with a man who could barely bring himself to say he loved her, who never told her she looked nice, and who once gave her a birthday card with a sticky note inside that simply read *Birthday*, because this way it could be recycled and used again. She remembers the year before she decided to leave as one filled with a storm of emotions: crying, pleading and yelling, all in service of the not unreasonable hope that he might 'be nice to me'. She had entered her thirties having absorbed the lessons of her twenties—that one must live as unobtrusively as possible in order to secure love, to be 'the sort of cool girl who does not have so many inconvenient needs'. And so she committed herself to this way of being, growing smaller and smaller in scope until she was left with only one need, the smallest of all but seemingly the hardest for him to fulfil: the need for him 'to notice things about how I was living'.

Having left my own small and unobserved life not long before this, I told the Bad Texter how deeply I related to the story and all the painful, wounding truths it laid bare about how we live and what we settle for. I implored him to read it, extolling its virtues as a piece of writing and an insight into the world of women in general, while not saying what it was I really meant: that *I* had needs too, just like this woman and her cranes. They weren't small and unimportant, and nor was I.

'It's not very long,' I assured him, having learned in my twenties the same lessons Hauser did about stepping gently through the time of men we like. He promised he would read it, and I felt another rusty cog loosen within me. We could be the kinds of people who read things together, not just for the things themselves but because of how the reading of them can help you to know a person.

When his phone pinged, he said he thought it might be his friends texting to let him know what they thought.

'As expected,' he said, looking down at the group chat on the screen. 'They think you're great. *Very pro Clem*, Andie says.'

I blushed, relieved and pleased. It felt good to be approved of, and I felt the compliment of it keenly. To be recognised as worthy in front of the object of your desire is always welcome, and when our waiter approached us moments later to say he was a fan of my work and wanted to pay for my wine as a gesture of gratitude, I offered up a silent prayer of thanks to whichever of the gods was looking out for my interests that night. What good fortune, to have your lover be told by both friends and strangers that you are a person who might be worth keeping around.

It must have had some kind of effect, because when we left the bar he pushed me against the wall and kissed me, whispering to me in a voice I hadn't heard before, as if it had been caught somewhere far below a dark swell and had only now found its way to the surface. My heart pounded again as I kissed him back, and other parts of me pounded too, the parts that had been pulled down into that deep ocean of desire.

I went home feeling once again like this might be the start of something significant. I spent the next few days in a dreamy reverie, allowing myself to imagine the full evolution of a love affair. Not just the friends we would meet and then share, but the stories too. The inside jokes, the shorthand we would develop to communicate, the trips we would take, the fights we would have (because there are always fights to be had when you're in love), the confessions shared. I thought about what it would look like if we fell in love, which surely we would. Who would say it first? Would it seem terrifying, in its naked vulnerability, or would saying it feel like the safest, most natural thing in the world? I considered the possibilities, holding them in the palm of my hand and gently caressing them as the world around me expanded in colours and sounds.

But as it happens, I was never invited to spend time with his friends again and I was too proud to bring myself to ask why. Perhaps it was the hair, after all.

❣

Maybe if we'd had uninterrupted time together, I might not have been so wildly off base about our prospects. But both of our jobs took us interstate regularly, which made it difficult to line up our schedules. I had joked to him in the beginning that we were like two ships passing in the night, but this became increasingly true as time wore on and the lightness with which the joke had first been made became heavier with each repetition, a skipping stone turned into a brick. We soon fell into a pattern in which we would see each other once a fortnight or so, after which I would intermittently delete his number from my phone and curse his name to the two friends who could still stand to hear me talking about him.

Mine was a problem as old as time itself: I had let myself like him, and in doing so lost all power over the situation. Shakespeare would have it that my heart had flown to his service, which in modern parlance is to say I had stupidly gone and 'caught feelings'. I was lovesick, and it seemed like nothing I did could shake the fever from me, nor the soul-wrenching ache that came from knowing he hadn't been similarly afflicted.

My phone became a weapon of mass distraction. Every time it beeped, I would get a little flutter of excitement at the possibility it could be him. It mostly wasn't, which was always a disappointment. But on the rare occasion it was, the alert popping up with whatever name it was I had him changed to that day, any distress that had been slowly building in me would instantly dissipate. I read and reread his texts, poring over them for clues as to the true nature of his feelings. *What does he mean by this?!* I'd fret, treating each benign joke and lengthy diatribe like the hint in a cryptic crossword puzzle.

I cannot explain exactly what it was that compelled me so deeply; I can only say I was like an addict waiting for a fix, resolving in each dry period to kick the habit and then falling into the sweet warmth of its embrace the moment it reappeared again. I felt like Frances, in Sally Rooney's *Conversations with Friends*, who describes the terrible existential pain of being ignored by the one you love as a 'shallow misery, which at any time could have been relieved completely by a word from him and transformed into idiotic happiness'.

I was thoroughly repulsed by my own behaviour. I knew logically that the temple I had erected inside my head for him to live in rent-free was ostentatiously grand, but I couldn't bring myself to dismantle it. I tried to send a wrecking ball through its belly, to have stern words with myself and to remember who I was and what I stood for, but all attempts proved futile. A friend told me it was too early in the piece to be feeling this powerless and I wanted to listen, I truly did. The problem was I wanted him even more, and I couldn't find a way to undo that.

In her review of Lisa Taddeo's book *Three Women*, the writer Francesca Giacco observes: 'The people who consume us the most, who inspire that kind of insane, untenable love, they're never really people, not entirely. They're ideas, aspirations, hurdles we'll never clear, but at the same time we can touch them, talk to them, absorb them. They take in and appreciate our nakedness, literal and otherwise. They earn our nervous trust.'

Of Maggie—one of the three women whose testimonies of desire are explored in Taddeo's book—Giacco writes: '[She] is in love with her teacher in that beautiful, shallow way we can be when we don't really know someone. But maybe you know some clue, like their favourite song, and you listen to it, trying to imagine them, the untold riches of their life before you knew them, and summon some ghost.'

As time wore on, I found myself obsessing in just this way over a man who had ceased in my mind to be someone made of flesh and blood and had instead morphed into an idea or outline.

Like Maggie, I had a series of clues about him and nothing but the strength of my own imagination and inescapable longing to try to fill in the gaps that connected them. Some days I thought of him as a punishment. Others, I extolled his virtues as a person of profound intellect and rakish good humour, a man who could delight me with a single shrewd word or self-effacing joke. In all respects he seemed to me a puzzle to be solved, but the more entangled I became in the pieces, the further away I got from being able to put them together.

He once told me that he hadn't had many serious relationships. It was an intimate confession, one I imagined had been made with me inside the metaphorical room in which secrets are exchanged and bonds are established. In being trusted with the information, I made the mistake of believing I would somehow surpass it. That I would join that small and exclusive group of women who had managed not just to glimpse the inner sanctum, but been invited to recline therein. It took me some time to realise that the confession might not have been so much an invitation as it was a gentle warning.

One evening, in a low and sullen mood, I spent a good ten or twenty minutes looking through his ex-girlfriend's social media accounts in order to compare myself unfavourably to her. I saw immediately that she was prettier than me, thinner and smaller and blessed by all the accompanying physical attributes we're taught to recognise as desirable in women. Even more egregiously, she was clearly smart and very politically driven. A brilliant, passionate activist with perfectly tousled hair, who may or may not have had a fiery temper but would still always be beautiful enough to get away with being angry.

Perhaps I should be ashamed to admit to something like this. But I know this sort of thing is familiar to many of us and brings with it the kind of masochistic pleasure that's made worse and therefore better by the performance of it all. Consequently, I was both disappointed and thrilled by the discovery, and repeated the activity numerous times over the next few weeks until its enjoyments became fewer and farther between and were eventually replaced by a dull, monotonous ache whose temper never varied.

❦

Spring arrived, bringing with it pockets of sunshine, longer days and the scent of jasmine on the breeze. I went to England for a month on a book tour, and spent far too much of the time wondering what he was doing. From the windows of trains moving between cities, from London to Oxford and Manchester to Birmingham, I stared out at rolling countryside and willed him to contact me. He texted me most days, but even though our conversations were sometimes long and far-reaching (and he seemed to enjoy the artfully shot photographs I'd also sent of me reclined in my underwear), he never said the one thing I wanted to hear: *I miss you.*

When I wasn't working, I distracted myself with long walks through East London, sometimes riding the tube to other parts of the city and making my way back on foot. I went on a date with a man from Tinder, a consultant for the NHS who taught me the sinister term 'deconditioning', but who also pulled me to him as we walked from one pub to another and kissed me eagerly in the middle of the cobblestoned streets. I slept with him a few nights later and enjoyed the experience, but when it was over I felt oppressed by the weight of his arm over my body and the feeling of his skin pressed against me, and wished only for him to leave. I saw him once more, when he took me to visit Benjamin Waterhouse Hawkins' famed dinosaur sculptures in Crystal Palace. He was entertaining and funny, but I politely declined the offer to go back to his house and pretended that I had made dinner plans with a friend. Riding home on the train, I pulled up a photo of the two of us standing in front of one of the misshapen sculptures and sent it to the Bad Texter with a caption joking about the 'weird old dinosaurs' we'd just seen, although of course what I was really saying was: *Other men find me attractive, you know.*

How can I have been so consumed? With so many hours in the day and so many rich experiences and opportunities to be distracted by, how can I have spent so much of it thinking about a single person?

But, then, we've all been there. Caught in the rusty trap of desire, unwilling to chew through a limb because to sever it means to lose it forever. And so, instead, I licked around the wound and ignored the many ways it could sting. *This is fine*, I kept telling myself as the blood oozed out. *It's barely a scratch.*

Before I knew it, my book tour was over and I was making the long journey home. I would see him in a matter of hours, and I turned over the prospect of this in my mind again and again. Each new scenario differed from the one before it only very slightly, an infinite number of possibilities forming the frames of an extremely sad, extremely boring stop animation in my head.

And then he was in front of me, sitting in the booth of a whisky bar with some friends. Conscious of the company, I gave him a chaste kiss hello, took a seat and tried to summon the kind of confident charm I thought might suit a woman who had just returned from a fancy work trip (to *London*, no less!) but I felt awkward and uncertain. I had landed less than six hours earlier, but the trip was already a distant memory. I had willed it away even while in the thick of it, but now that I had arrived in the moment I'd been imagining for weeks I wasn't sure how to act or even how to *be*. I felt that familiar insecurity wrap itself around me, the terrible feeling of being too much of the things people didn't like and not enough of the things they did. Jet-lagged, and with the effects of the Valium I always take when flying still coursing through my veins, I became horribly inebriated and we had the kind of sex that would be forgettable were the memory of your mortifying attempts to be 'sexy' not burned into your brain and ready to be replayed forevermore.

Still on London time, I woke early the next morning feeling hungover and embarrassed. He was asleep next to me but lying a canyon's distance away, and I felt every last metaphorical mile keenly. The thought that he might wake up and sense the uncomfortably charged energy in the room made me feel sick. It was one thing for *me* to notice how terribly askew things seemed between us. I had a lifetime of practice in swallowing discomfort and pretending everything was okay. But I couldn't predict or control how he would respond, and the thought of him finding me too difficult or unpleasant to be around was more than I could bear. I wanted him to leave because that way I could preserve whatever lies I had been telling myself about the situation; but I wanted him to stay too, because I loved him, or at least wanted the chance for that to be true.

I was prickly and on edge by the time he woke up, and consequently felt the need to apologise. He had an appointment, but we arranged to meet for brunch later at a cafe in Fitzroy. The uncomfortable electric feeling stayed with me through the morning, making me feel defensive and annoyed by the time I sat in the booth opposite him. Gone was the lightness of those early dates, replaced with what felt to me like strange formalities and that telltale storm brewing inside that told me I was gearing up for a fight. He dropped me to my car when we'd finished eating, and once again I felt overcome by the need to apologise—although whether this was for something specific or my existence in general was unclear.

The problem, I realised, was that we were floating in that strange liminal space between casually dating and properly seeing someone. Defining the relationship would give me the answers I needed, and so I texted him later that night and laid my cards on the table.

Hey there, I began. *I think I was a little awkward and weird today because I'm not really sure what's going on. I hate to do this over text but I guess I'm just looking for some indication of what our boundaries are. Like, should we be seeing other people? Not seeing other people? No need to answer straight away, I just really wanted to put it out there.*

He replied straight away. *I'm unsure about all these things too. I'd much prefer we discuss it in person though rather than over text. Can we speak when I get back from interstate? I'm glad you brought it up.*

It was a positive response, warm and inviting, and I felt some of my anxiety about the situation ease. The only problem, once again, was timing. I would be heading to Bali for a writers' festival before he came home, which meant it would be another three weeks before we could have this important in-person talk.

Two ships in the night! I joked again.

The two ships thing doesn't help, Clem! he replied.

And no, I suppose it didn't.

❣

Bali came and went, but the passage of time alleviated none of the tedious obsession that was plaguing me. By the time we managed to see each other again, almost four weeks had passed since I'd returned from London.

We met at the wine bar again, the same one in which I had asked his permission to touch him and felt his hands clasp mine in response. I didn't have the same confidence this time, and so I sat with my hands folded in my lap. We chatted lightly about this and that, neither of us acknowledging what we had ostensibly met to discuss and yet feeling it there like a third wheel, all the same. It wasn't until later, after we'd paid the bill and walked the short distance to his house, that the topic was raised.

'So,' he said, pulling me into the crook of his arm as we lay back against his pillows. 'Shall we talk?'

'Sure,' I replied casually, as if I hadn't instigated this whole thing.

I repeated what I had said to him almost a month earlier: that I was looking for some indication of what our obligations to each other were. He told me he had just signed another contract with his employer, and he was committed to fulfilling it in a way that would make a relationship basically impossible. Because of that, he wouldn't want to stop me from dating other people.

I agreed this was sensible, making sure to emphasise that I was also very busy and that of course I had a child to think about too, which made my own schedule impossible to wrangle. We lay there in silence for a minute, before I suddenly spoke up.

'Just to be clear,' I said, 'I wasn't asking you to be my *boyfriend* or anything.'

'No, of course not,' he replied. 'I didn't think you were!'

Reader, I was lying. *Obviously.*

What is the purpose of a lie like this, when it only brings you more hurt in the long run? Like so many women of my generation (and perhaps like so many women of *all* generations) I felt constrained by my own fear of what it meant to ask for exactly what I wanted, because I knew the likelihood of getting it was slim to none. I could scrunch my needs into a tiny ball and bury them deep in the dirt until even I had forgotten where they were and what they looked like. I could be happy, if I just adjusted my expectations.

Haven't we all found ourselves in this situation? Sweeping crumbs into the palms of our hands, telling ourselves that it doesn't really matter how much someone gives us to eat because we're not that hungry anyway?

No more for me, thanks. I'm all full up!

I left that night having technically resolved the issue but feeling just as troubled as before. Later, as I was drifting off to sleep, I recalled a conversation we'd had before I'd left for London, when he came over to watch a movie and I tentatively asked him if he'd like to stay the night.

'But you don't have to,' I qualified quickly.

He laughed. 'I know,' he said. 'You always say that!'

'Yes, because I somehow manage to always feel really uncool around you,' I replied, being unexpectedly candid for a moment.

'Don't be silly,' he said. 'You're cool!'

'I know,' I said, turning to look at him pointedly, a sharp edge to my voice.

The act felt brazen but familiar, as if I'd been sucked under a wave and had glimpsed a former version of myself silhouetted in the light above the surface. *Come back! Come back!* she called down to me. But then she was gone, and I was floating in the swell alone again.

❦

We trundled along with nothing of importance happening between us until suddenly something did. It was the last time I saw him before we properly 'broke up', if you can use that term to describe people who've defined the relationship as Not One. By chance, we both happened to be interstate at the same time, and I invited him to stay with me at my hotel. I was arriving late at night, and he texted me as I was driving into the city.

Remind me where the place is again?

I gave him the address and told him if it was too late that was fine, and that I could just see him the next day. I had flattened myself almost completely by this stage, as thin as the piece of paper one might use to fold an origami crane, one whose feathers had all been plucked just as Hauser had told it.

No, no! he replied. *It's actually very convenient for me, because it's close to work.*

Just what every girl wants to hear! I joked.

I was sitting up in bed when he arrived, having practised a number of 'casual' poses. He climbed in next to me, and we did what we had always done best—talked for hours about this, that and the other.

My event was the following night, so I spent the morning taking some suggestive photographs for him in an attempt to stoke whatever flames there might be left. His response was encouraging (*Wear that tonight, and only that*), and I thought the trip might just reinvigorate something between us after all. I was hosting a dinner and panel for a group of women in the hotel's fancy restaurant, which should have been enough to breathe some confidence back into me and remind me who I was in the world. But this isn't how things work, particularly not for women, and so I hinged all of my feelings of self-worth that day on whether or not he would appreciate the dress I was wearing, and if he would like the way my legs looked in sky-high heels well enough to want to peel them apart.

Not really, as it turned out.

I met him in the lobby of the hotel just after the dinner had finished ('You're so tall in those shoes!' was all he said), and we took a punishing elevator ride to the fourth floor. I waited for him to express some enthusiasm when we had finally made it into the room, but he just walked across to the bed, stripped down to his boxers and t-shirt and climbed under the blankets. I stood there awkwardly in the tall heels and the daring dress before unzipping myself, trying my best not to stumble or appear any more ridiculous than I already felt. I grabbed a singlet and disappeared into the bathroom to brush my teeth and put on a more comfortable pair of underwear, because the thought of him seeing the effort I'd gone to was almost more humiliating than not being touched at all.

And then we lay there talking once again, as devoid of spark as an old married couple discussing the boring ins and outs of the day. Except that even this implies an intimacy of some kind, and there was none of that there. I was filled once again with the desire for him to leave, and yet I couldn't bring myself to voice it out loud because I knew that would mark the absolute end of it all. I was prepared to let it limp to the finish line, because a grim and pallid love with him still seemed at that point to be better than none at all.

Instead, I kissed him. Small kisses, inviting kisses, the kind of kisses two people might share if they were lying in bed together in a room paid for by someone else. He pulled me to him as if welcoming the gesture, but offered so little in the way of response immediately afterwards that I gave up and retreated back to my own side of the bed, putting as much distance between me and his rigid body as possible.

(Sidenote: This is why arguments about consent and 'confusing non-verbal signals' are so infuriating. Because you *know* when someone doesn't want you near them, you *know* when the feel of your lips on theirs is met with revulsion. No one can have felt those things and claimed not to know, because there is no more obvious feeling in the world than sensing the tension in someone's body as they will you to stop touching them.)

'I'm sorry,' he said to me. 'I'm just so tired.'

Why did you come here then? I wanted to ask. Not because I expected him to sleep with me and certainly not because I felt like I was owed it in any way. But perhaps even worse than the feeling of rejection is the feeling that one is an obligation. I had given him numerous opportunities to avoid a scenario just like this one, and the fact he had chosen to put us both in it anyway was a kind of cruelty or, worse, thoughtlessness that I couldn't get my head around.

I woke early the next morning, after a tense and uncomfortable sleep. I was on the red-eye flight back to Melbourne, and as I tiptoed quietly around the room in the darkness of the pre-dawn I sensed he was awake too. But he kept his eyes closed and stayed still, and only shifted when I bent down to kiss him goodbye, as if he had been caught in the middle of a dream and not engaged in the concentrated determination we have all had at some point to pass undetected by a lover we no longer want.

❣

A week or so later, the me that had been stuck below the swell finally broke through the surface. I was drinking with some friends in the late summer sun, and one of them very gently mentioned she had seen him on one of the dating apps. I waved her concern away, saying it wasn't a big deal. We weren't in a relationship and, besides, I was also swiping and dating, so I could hardly be upset.

But I was. I was!

I realised, finally, that I had found myself stuck in the cliché that plagues all of us at one point or another: I was waiting for him to change his mind. I was that meme of the cartoon dog, sitting in a room on fire with a dopy grin on its face, saying, 'This is fine!'

But it wasn't. It wasn't!

I knew that I was a stopgap. I had known it for a long time, but as the sun moved across the sky that afternoon and the shadows grew long, I finally admitted it to myself. I wasn't the destination. I was just a detour on the way to something better; an okay enough town to pass through but a place whose delights could only stretch so far.

And of course, I absorbed his lack of interest as my own failing. I had always wanted to be the kind of woman who revealed more of herself with each layer unwrapped, but perhaps I was the opposite. Perhaps the more someone discovered of me, the less interesting I became.

I didn't want to be wallpaper in the background of someone's life, but if I continued in this way that's exactly what I would allow myself to become. He could do the soft fade, slowly but surely peeling me away until there was nothing but the barest trace of me left, a memory of a pattern that had existed there once but had long been without form or function. Or I could tear the damn wrapping off myself.

I tore.

I drafted a text message to him later that night, a howl of anger that unleashed all the emotions I'd restrained since meeting him, terrified as I was that he might discover I had needs that required tending. I told him, among other wounded sentiments offered, that it was clear he had no respect for me, and that we might as well end things right now.

He replied urgently the next morning, asking if we could meet to talk. I agreed to meet him and the dog, the one with the proud ears, for a walk along the creek. A part of me wanted to retract everything I'd said, to swallow it all back down along with my pride. But I knew this wasn't the answer, and it never had been.

We exchanged some minor chatter before he turned to me and said, 'So. Your text.'

'Ha, yes!' I replied, still wanting in some way to seem like an agreeable person. 'I was pretty angry.'

'But we talked about this,' he said. 'I told you I wasn't looking for a relationship right now because I'm so busy with work.'

'Yes,' I replied again, more seriously this time. 'But this isn't about a relationship. Whether someone sees me one day a month or seven days a week, I'd like to feel like they actually *want* to be there.'

I told him how humiliated I had felt after the scene in the hotel room, and how awful it was to feel like someone was repulsed by your touch.

'It felt like I was assaulting you,' I said, the humiliation flooding me once more.

He looked genuinely pained, and apologised.

'It's true what I said,' he began. 'I really am extremely exhausted right now. But the thing is, kissing and canoodling and so on, it's very intimate. And I didn't want to confuse things, given we'd talked about not being in a relationship.'

So you can fuck me, I thought, *but you can't kiss me?*

'I understand all that,' I said. 'I just don't understand why you came to the room in the first place. I would never want anyone to feel obliged to me in any way, but two people who have sex but aren't in a relationship don't go to a hotel room to lie rigidly next to each other because they're afraid of *confusing* things. I feel like I gave you numerous opportunities to decline the invitation. Why didn't you?'

'Because I like talking to you!' he said, as if that explained the matter.

'Yes, we've always been very good at that, haven't we?' I replied, and I was good humoured about it.

We walked in silence for a few more moments.

'I guess part of what I find confusing is that it started out with so much promise,' I said. 'In the beginning, it really felt like we were opening up to each other.' I stopped on the path to look at him. I wasn't angry anymore, just sad. 'I feel as if you invited me into your house, waited until I got to the top of the stairs and then slammed the door in my face. But instead of sending me away you just kept me waiting there, on the porch.'

'That's good.' He laughed. 'Are you some kind of writer or something?'

I smiled.

'I think we should probably not see each other at all for a while,' he said, serious now. 'Otherwise, I'll keep inviting you back to that porch, because I enjoy your company.'

'Yes,' I said, still smiling. 'I think that's probably a wise idea.'

We walked some more, circling down to one of the playgrounds along the creek's trail. Our conversation returned to the things we had always covered so well together—politics, ideas, all of the strange and weird things that constituted my life as an online personality. But as we sat on the park's swings and slowly swayed in the breeze, I returned to the subject at hand.

'Do you think things would have been different?' I asked him. 'If circumstances had been different, I mean?'

'I don't know,' he replied cautiously. 'If we had time together uninterrupted by work and life, then maybe we could have seen what was there.'

'No,' I said, throwing open the locked box that protected both my ego and my vulnerability. 'I mean, am I the kind of person that you'd want to be with?'

'Oh, well, yes!' he said, with more enthusiasm. 'You're smart and funny. You're also a ratbag and I like that about you. And you actually have a trait that I think is rare in a lot of people and that most people wouldn't expect of you, which is that you're willing to change your mind on things.'

I looked down at the tanbark and smiled.

No, I thought to myself. *You're still not listening. What I really want to know is: do you think I'm pretty?*

❦

We said goodbye in the car park, and then I went home and did all the things you're supposed to do when your heart suffers a small wound. I cried a little. I drank a lot. I pined. I dabbled in witchcraft, casting spells and rituals that would help me to sever the connection I was still tending to in my heart. I resisted the urge to text him, almost breaking my resolve once or twice or maybe ten times before Andie ('Very pro Clem' Andie, with whom I'd become excellent friends, proving once again that the best thing to come out of break-ups with men is friendships with women) suggested I open a note on my phone and just write all my texts to him there. They live on forever now, in the Cloud.

> How was your flight?
> You should watch this trailer about austerity in the UK.
> Trump impeached!
> We should not ignore each other anymore, because I
> don't like it.
> Who are you talking to on WhatsApp all those times
> that I can see you've been online?
> You really should watch *Years and Years*.
> Why didn't you want me?

I can read them now without feeling pained or embarrassed, instead recognising them for what they are: proof of life. My year of desperate yearning is evidence that even someone like me, a hardline feminist with an inherent distrust of men and all their motives, is capable of great feeling. It is not love that compels us to keep trying. It is hope.

❣

Writing this has been difficult not because it pains me to revisit the situation but because it is so *tedious* to wade through the memories of a thwarted love affair. Every word, every movement, every action is catalogued in real time with fastidious devotion and kept in perpetuity in an archive. But now that I am coming to the conclusion, I feel released.

So here is the ending . . . Eventually I recovered, and the Bad Texter and I became friends. Proper friends, without subterfuge or artifice. I no longer scour his words for hidden meanings or spend hours analysing his behaviour. He exists, I exist, and sometimes those things happen in the same place and at the same time.

It began with texts, casual enquiries about our respective lives peppered by the kind of shrewd observations and bon mots we had always been so good at. He added me on Facebook and followed me on Instagram, because now that the threat of confusing sexual intimacy was gone we could share and grow an actual platonic intimacy without fear.

We hung out in cinemas and over dinners, and although my hands were tense at first and I was unsure what to do with them, even they thawed after a while and began to find their natural rhythm again.

We met recently to see a movie.

I was standing at the top of the escalator when he arrived, looking at my phone. We said hello and headed down the stairs to the cinema bar. In another of his devotions to extremity, he had decided to give up drinking for three months, so we ordered a pot of herbal tea each and went to sit on the balcony.

I was thrilled again by how easy and enjoyable conversation was between the two of us, but there was something else this time. A lightness in me, a lack of uncertainty about where I stood. We were just two friends, sitting on a balcony on a midsummer evening, enjoying a cup of tea and making each other laugh.

The movie itself was beautiful, a sparse love story about two men, seemingly strangers, who meet in Barcelona only for one of them to realise what the other has known all along—that they have met once before, when they were young men on the cusp of adulthood. It's atmospheric and raw, and there are some exceptionally hot sex scenes. But there's also a sequence towards the end, when one of the men experiences a waking dream depicting what might have happened had their first brief encounter turned into something more significant. It's a sliding door moment, a chance to explore the 'what if?' that haunts almost every love affair.

What if we had stayed together? What if we had built a life? What kind of food would we have in our fridge, what would our baby look like, what would it be like to have sex with each other after so many years of familiarity?

As quickly as it's introduced, the moment is gone and reality reasserts itself. There are two men, one standing on a balcony and one looking up at it, and in the short line of space between them and the look they share lie infinite possibilities.

We agreed the movie was wonderful and discussed this and other things over a final cup of tea. He walked me to my bike and we hugged goodbye, promising to meet soon for a picnic because, as he said, 'you're always going on about those!'.

I laughed. 'Well, I'm very good at them!'

I rode home through the quiet streets, the damp breeze causing me to shiver. As I pedalled, I thought of those infinite possibilities that exist for us all. Not just between two people— although of course there is that too—but the endless doors we have the opportunity to walk through, that lead us down hallways and through castles and caverns and attics to find different doors, and how we walk and walk and walk, choosing to pick up some things on the way but not others, and how in the end this is what it means to assemble a life. I thought of how when you meet some people it's as if you have met them before, in a time or a moment you can't quite grasp, like a song whose melody eludes you, a dream whose wispy edges dance on the edges of your memory.

I thought of how I had been trapped in the feeling of wanting him for so long that I hadn't really seen him at all. I thought of how I had taken the promise of him and buried myself inside it, making myself smaller and smaller in the hope he wouldn't mind that I was there.

The sickness of love entered my body with the force of a thunderclap, but when it left it was quietly, like the receding tide. I had been flooded with it for so long that I didn't notice at first, but one day I looked up to realise I was standing on dry land and the waves that had been pulling at me were now far off in the distance. I knew they would return, but he wouldn't be there with them. He was somewhere else, standing on his own shore, being battered by the wind and the water and whatever siren's song he was haunted by.

Instead, the waves would carry with them the promise of someone new, a different person with a different form who would grip me with that same familiar fever and ecstasy and consume my waking dreams. And after them it would be someone else, and someone else, and someone else. I didn't know any of them yet, but I could see them lined up along the horizon, waiting. All of these infinite possibilities of love to explore, to learn from, to grieve and to rejoice in. Some of them would hurt me and some of them would heal me. And my heart would be big enough to hold them all.

My goodness! How much there is to look forward to!

7

THE WALKING HEART

To give birth, whether at home in a birth tub with candles
and family or in a surgical suite with machines and a neonatal
team, a woman must go to the place between this world and
the next, to that thin membrane between here and there.
To the place where life comes from, to the mystery, in order
to reach over to bring forth the child that is hers.

Jana Studelska, 'The Last Days of Pregnancy: A Place of In-Between'

When I was fifteen or so, I arrived home one day to find a baby
bird that had fallen out of its nest. It was writhing slowly on
our driveway, and so new was it that its eyes were still sealed
shut. I picked it up carefully and carried it inside cradled in the
palm of my hand. I knew nothing about birds or even animal

care in general, but I was excited at the thought of pulling off some kind of veterinary feat.

I'll save you, I tried to communicate psychically to the bird.

I found a small cardboard box and filled it with cotton wool, reasoning (probably incorrectly) that a freshly born baby bird would like to recuperate in something soft. I lay the bird in there and cooed at it for a minute or two before I lost interest and disappeared into my room.

An hour or so later, I returned to the kitchen to play with my new pet. It was chirping faintly, and I scooped it out carefully to hold in my hand once again, stroking its soft head. Suddenly, I felt something wet on my hand and watched as a long stream of poo dropped out of the bird's bottom and into my palm.

'Urrrgh!' I exclaimed, flinging the bird away from me and watching as it hit the ground.

'Sorry, sorry, sorry!' I repeated over and over, picking the poor little thing up again and trying unsuccessfully to will it back to life.

I buried it outside in the garden and avoided looking at the spot for weeks afterwards.

This is an ugly memory. But, then, motherhood is full of them.

❣

Tell me a story, he says to her in bed one night, one arm wrapped around the floppy neck of his Teddy and the other curled around her elbow.

What story could one possibly tell from this vantage point, the place in which we stand when we stand at the end of the world? It is the beginning of the global pandemic, and nothing could capture the depth of feeling, the fear, the love, the dreams and the hope that they feel. The end of the world is nigh, the placards once told them, and they didn't believe them because seeing is believing, but here they are, seeing, and it seems impossible to believe. The end of the world.

Tell me a story.

They are bewildered, and the bewildered have never been good at remembering details.

Of course, it is not the end of the world, far from it. But they don't know that yet. The world itself will keep on turning, rolling through the universe at the same pace, trundling through time with the same maddening torpor that's caused us all, at one point or another, to sit on our beds or in our cars or just in our heads and scream dramatically (internally or otherwise), *I cannot wait a second longer for my life to begin!* The turning, rolling, trundling world that has at the same time torpedoed through space, tearing us up from infancy into adulting with a seemingly never-ending acceleration that sees us all standing there every March without fail, yawping at each other, 'Can you *believe* it's March already? *March!* My goodness, where on *earth* does the time go?!'

For now, time is on hold. She and her son are in lockdown, along with the rest of the world, and each day spills into the next with little variation and no end in sight.

But it's not the end of the world; the world will go on turning, rolling and trundling regardless, because the humans that live on it are ultimately superfluous to its existence. The simple fact of this is a source of both distress and relief. Distress because we are accustomed to positioning ourselves as central to anything and everything that happens around us, even (and perhaps especially) the entire history of the universe. But there is relief too, because the realisation that we are essentially meaningless sacks of flesh attached to a rock caught in the vacuum of space is a form of wonderful absolution. If anything, the planet will thrive in our absence. No more car fumes clogging up her airways. No more plastic discarded in the ocean. No more high-tension Christmases spent trying not to argue with family. The list of benefits is literally endless.

And yet. And yet.

We—humans, I mean—are attached to meaning and purpose above all else. And there is no greater meaning and purpose for us here, at the end of the world, than trying to figure out what the meaning and purpose of it all is, or was, or may still be.

Because maybe there may still be.

She hopes that there may still be. This virus may not have wiped us out, but what about everything that comes afterwards, when the virus has made a wreckage of all that we egotistically, arrogantly believed was above destruction? What a wonderful joke! After all that, it turned out to be the common cold, wielded by us—humans, I mean—in our own drawing rooms.

Of course, there is so much more to come. This is not the end of the world, not even for humans. But she doesn't know that yet, because it feels very much like her world is ending. She doesn't know that one day she'll be able to look back and feel distanced from the fear, the suffocation, the dread terror of waking up each day to experience the same thing on repeat.

I am in that moment now, the one she didn't know then was coming, and I want to reach out to that version of me and hold her. I want to tell her it will all be okay. I want to tell her that good things are coming, that relief is on its way. But even if I could, none of that would change the fact that the only way to *this* point in time is to go through *all that* time.

And so I watch her, in my memory. She sits in her living room with a child who is not old enough to understand any of this, or to comprehend how this wreckage might have been wrought by our own hands. He asks for peanut butter sandwiches for breakfast and then again for lunch, with the express request they be cut into triangles. He eats them in small bites while watching episode after episode of his favourite cartoon on the television, because she long ago abandoned the idea that she would 'never use TV as a babysitter!'. Afterwards, he runs around nude with no thoughts of modesty, because he has yet to learn that his body must be a source of either pride or shame but never neutrality. She wonders how long it will be until she's no longer allowed to see those parts of him, and even though she knows this is correct and how it must be, there is a part of her that mourns how time can take from us just as much as it gives.

'Mummy, can we make the funny faces?' he asks, smiling toothily. He means the filtered lenses they've found together on various photo apps, the ones that render him bearded or bespectacled or monster-like or turn him into a dog. She looks up from her phone and the Very Serious Government Updates she's been listening to while she sits there on the balcony, hot cup of coffee nestled between her thighs and worry on her mind. She considers his request.

Tell me a story, he is asking.

Tell me a story. As if we need more stories. As if the world isn't full of the weight and detritus of human stories, the damage we have done and the harm we have caused. As if the world isn't full of human hubris and our unstinting belief that the most fortunate among us—the wealthy, the long-limbed, the well situated, the privileged—are also the most worthy and, deceptively, the *most interesting.*

Tell me a story. As if there could ever be enough stories to reflect what it means for any of us to be human and alive, to be sacks of flesh capable of the most exquisite crafting of poetry and prose, lines that make us weep with longing, phrases that make us shiver with desire, as if the breath of another human were right there on the nape of our neck, coaxing us into life. As if we could ever properly articulate what it means to breathe in the particular scent of your child, to listen as they laugh in their sleep, to feel the guilt of wanting them to leave us alone even as we yearn for them to never leave us at all. As if there could ever be enough *words* to capture what it means to love and desire and want and need and sacrifice and give and take and feel pain and feel hope and feel anger and feel panic and feel like it has never been enough, like none of it will ever be enough, like there is not enough time, there is not enough time, there is not enough time because this is it, it's happening right now and although it has taken us an eternity to get here we understand at last that. there. is. not. enough. time.

'Mummy,' he asks again, 'can we please make the funny faces?'

'Of course we can, my darling,' she replies, putting her coffee down and pulling him into her lap.

She thinks the world is ending. And because she thinks this means the stories will end too, she tells him the ones she already knows.

❣

In the early days of our courtship, before domestic cohabitation and pregnancy, before the screaming fights, the frustration and the slow boil of resentment filtered in through the cracks that our love and care had never been able to properly seal, my son's father and I went out on a late summer evening for a romantic stroll. We were holding hands and laughing, entirely carefree save for the gentle thrum of anticipation that accompanies any budding romance. Ahead of us, a car was parked with its passenger doors open. Someone—the driver, presumably—was attempting to wrestle a bar fridge into the car's rear.

'Woah, I can help you with that!' I called out, dropping the hand of my new lover and sprinting forward. 'You get on the other side and I'll push it through to you as you pull it into place.'

The fridge wasn't that heavy and I lifted it easily, manoeuvring it into place and sliding it along the back seat. It only took a minute, no more than two, and I stood up afterwards, grinning and satisfied. My beau watched from the sidewalk laughing.

'You just threw that thing in there like it was no big deal!' he marvelled.

'Oh, it was nothing,' I said, brushing off the compliment but smiling broadly as I basked in the warm glow of his admiration. I was falling in love with him, and I was glad he had been there to witness what I assumed was one of my most compelling and attractive qualities: that I am more than capable of taking care of myself.

The accumulation of both years and experience has taught me that most men do not consider this trait to be desirable in the women they might want to sleep with. But J___ did. Even now, he'll tell the story to anyone who'll listen, and the light that was there all those years ago on that summer evening still dances somewhere in his eyes.

Although the parameters of our particular story have changed, I hold on to this moment—this other person's *memory* of me—as a kind of powerful talisman. I am a capable woman. I am strong. I can throw a fridge into the back of a car all by myself. Life could be tackled in much the same way, careening between tasks big and small and flexing the muscles that were needed, and this was both as simple and as complicated as it ever needed to be.

I threw myself into the prospect of motherhood in much the same way, with little thought beyond it being something I thought I wanted to do, or at least wanted to have others *watch* me doing. I had decided I wanted a baby, we stuck the landing on the first try, and I set about waiting for everything else to slide neatly into place. I didn't think about it in any great depth beyond this, and why should I have? I was throwing a fridge into the back of a car in front of a handful of spectators, some of whom would look at me with admiration because I had made it seem easy.

Oh, it's nothing! I would say. *Really. You just have to take a deep breath and remember to bend at the knees.*

Months later, after a birth that left my body torn and bruised, my throat and chest aching from the fire that ignites when you scream a baby into the world, I lay in our bed with the tiny creature curled up next to me and had a sudden, panicked realisation about the permanency of the situation.

I've made a terrible mistake, I thought.

The thought was gone as quickly as it had appeared, some deeper maternal instinct pushing it back into the darkness, keeping it at bay so as to protect me from the gnashing of its razor-sharp teeth. But I could feel it lurking there, its eyes on me, waiting for the moment to strike.

I can catch a glimpse of it even now, in the right light.

❦

Sometime at the beginning of autumn, when the weather is still good and the prospect of the pandemic making its way to Australia seems less like a vague possibility and more like a nightmarish certainty, when people in her own suburb begin hoarding toilet paper and pasta and giant bags of flour (the latter seeming odd for a neighbourhood boasting approximately three artisanal bakeries to every one resident, which indicates a general lack of interest in baking for oneself), when people begin having fretful conversations on the street and in cafes about how nervous they are and how it's all terrible, just *terrible*, when rumours are being whispered of the Melbourne Pavilion and the Showgrounds being turned into triage centres and makeshift morgues, and when, as a result of all this, a nationwide lockdown seems imminent, she buys a new bicycle.

Her old bicycle had been stolen a month or so earlier from outside the North Fitzroy Library. She'd left it there after getting drunk one night with Alice in the nearby gardens. They'd been writing in the library, each of them slogging their way towards their daily word counts, occasionally looking up at each other with pained faces to express how much they loathed the task of writing, and how they were absolute fools for choosing a career in which they spent 90 percent of their working life hating themselves.

It was one of the last nights of summer, a Friday, and the gardens were full of people pleasure-seeking. Some of them were clustered in groups of two or three, clutching beer bottles or plastic wine cups. The air was still and warm, but there was a whisper of something in it that reminded them it wouldn't be like this for long. That soon the nights would begin earlier, the leaves would fall with the temperature and, before they knew it, winter would be upon them.

They couldn't know then that the winter would bring such a sense of foreboding, nor that their time of drinking wine together and breaking down the problems of the world was set to change drastically. Perhaps it's better that they didn't know, that they were able to enjoy a final summer evening together, delighting in each other's company.

But she was in a bad mood that night, and as it was she picked a fight with Alice about something silly—men, probably—and they ended the night feeling bitter and cross with one another. She was far too drunk to ride home, so she left the bicycle outside the library and allowed herself to be distracted from the task of collecting it for weeks, until someone else took care of the problem for her, which of course she'd known they would.

Not long after, she and Alice began preparing for the end of the world. Alice was better equipped for this task than she was, having spent the last eight or so years pondering the narrative possibilities presented by total societal collapse. Alice is what is known these days as a 'cli-fi' novelist, a writer of speculative fiction about a world arrested by climate change, in which humanity is confronted with the consequences of its own inaction. You know, light-reading-before-bed-type stuff.

Climate change. It seems like such a distant problem to them now! For a time, they joked this might be the world's attempt at repairing itself, bringing to a standstill the biggest pandemic and virus the planet had ever known: us, humanity, the whole stinking kit and caboodle of it all.

But though they may have been joking, still they reached for the evidence of it with earnest optimism. People love to find symbolism in the obstacles they encounter. A global pandemic couldn't possibly exist as a matter of random fact; there must be some kind of *meaning* attached to it. A reason for all this fear, anxiety and, let's be honest, inconvenient interruption.

Did you hear? they began announcing to each other excitedly, in between the fretful enquiries into one's mental health that had replaced normal greetings. *There are* dolphins *in the canals of Venice!*

Alice, who had been tracking the climate's grievances for so long that she considered it a matter of 'when' and not 'if' her fictional predictions would come true, found herself torn between hope for a future in which they weren't being sucked beneath floodwater or ravaged by fire, and despair at the fact that either way they were still saying goodbye to the world as they'd known it.

The panic buying had just started at this point, and although they weren't certain where it might lead, they knew how scenarios like this ended. They'd seen *Years and Years* only recently, for crying out loud! They laid out their what-if plans in hushed, guarded voices over dinner while the children played together, and devised back-up plans in the rapid-fire texts they sent to one another. *We could go to my mother's house in the country,* Alice wrote, *pitch tents in the garden and pretend to the children we're having an adventure.*

And after all, was this not exactly what they were having? An adventure, unexpected and unprecedented, but filled with its own rich narrative of possibilities? For amid the tension in the air, the anxiety about what was coming and the prospect that everything they had ever loved or pined for or even just taken for granted was about to end, there was something else too. A thrumming below the surface, a stirring, a deep vibration that signalled something *exciting* could be about to begin, even as everything else seemed set to end.

They were writers, she and Alice, and they had lived in the words on the page. They had suffered for them, bled for them, cried over them, been consumed by the tediousness of them but still, more than anything, they had thrilled in the possibility of life those words had created. They could survive what was coming by romanticising it; by becoming characters in their own real-life novel, each of them speaking their lines as if they had been written for them by a distant hand to whom they could also surrender the direction of the plot.

And so she buys a bicycle, sleek and black, with smooth gears and an electric boost that whirrs quietly as the pedals turn, with space at the back for a child's seat. They could travel easily on it, her and the boy, over back roads or under cover of night if they needed to.

It's sensible to have a means of escape when you don't know what's going to happen next. This is what she tells Alice, who agrees.

❣

Years ago, before my son was born, before I'd even settled on whether or not I wanted to have a child at all, I had a dream one night about a foundling. The baby was not mine but had come into my care for one reason or another. At first, I was inconvenienced by its presence. But I cared for it nonetheless, because it had no one else and could not care for itself.

At some point in the dream, my sense of what was happening shifted and the dream itself moved into more lucid territory. I remember looking at the baby, that unknown squalling thing, and being struck by the most primal sense of urgency.

I would die to protect you—and I knew it within myself rather than thought it, the words filling me like a balloon expanding suddenly from limp and deflated to round and full. It wasn't a promise or a bargain; it was a cold, hard fact.

I woke up with the memory of the foundling still swirling in my chest. *This must be what it feels like to be a mother,* I thought. To know without question that you would die to protect someone. That you would kill to defend them. And after all, isn't this what we're always told about motherhood? That it's raw and instinctual rather than a choice we must make every day, even when we are racked by grief for our former selves?

I leaned into this belief in the early weeks of my pregnancy, so thrilled was I at the thought of embarking on this glossy new project. I imagined myself lying in crisp white sheets, a gurgling ball of bliss lying peacefully next to me while a soft breeze drifted through the window. In my heavily filtered imagination, I was radiant. Motherhood would deliver me from the awkward insecurity I had felt my whole life and allow me to finally arrive into my true self. The act of a child crashing through me would be enough to shuck the last vestiges of ugly flesh from me; having been broken, I would emerge from my chrysalis, beautifully whole and wholly beautiful.

I clung to this belief even more fiercely when, at exactly twenty-four weeks plus two days pregnant, I was hit by a tidal wave of pre-natal anxiety so debilitating that I spent the next three months drowning beneath it. I had experienced terrifying bouts of anxiety before, since the first time I backflipped out of my own brain when I was just twelve years old to the months I spent at twenty feeling like I was living inside a glass jar and the time later on, at thirty-one, when I sat down on the couch one day and was gripped by the sudden fear that my existence itself was an elaborate illusion. Each of these descents into madness was marked by a constant, unrelenting terror, eclipsed only by the incredible loneliness that comes from feeling so lost. Finding my way back to the light had always been an arduous task, but the day always came when with one final heave I was able to drag myself back up to the surface and suck in great lungsful of air. *I survived!* I would marvel. *Look at how beautiful it is up here above the waves!*

But the madness of pregnancy was like nothing I'd experienced before. The threat to my wellbeing was no longer an existential crisis but the very real presence of a *thing* growing inside me. Nothing I could do would change the nature of the thing; it would keep growing until it was ready to come out, and this would involve a period of time in which I would simply need to endure.

For most of us, time is experienced in great chunks. We move through it with little attention paid to its mechanics, barely noticing as it delivers us from one moment to the next. But the darkest period of my pregnancy was spent in a state of hyper-awareness of time. Each minute was accounted for, the weight of it pressing on me just as the entity inside my body grew into the space meant for my organs. The refrain of time played in my head all day long: *fifteen weeks left, fifteen weeks left, fourteen weeks left, fourteen weeks left.* I imagined turning up to the hospital and demanding they remove the thing that was flopping about inside me like a bucket full of eels.

On the really bad days, I imagined doing it myself. Plunging a knife deep into my belly, ending the torment that had decimated my appetite and seen me waking at all hours of the night, stumbling to the balcony of our apartment building in the hope the cold air might calm my breaths. I saw myself doing it, standing in the kitchen one day or lying in the bath, and these thoughts would send me into a spiralling panic. I didn't *want* to hurt myself or even hurt the thing—but I was afraid that a time might come when I was depleted of the courage I needed to resist it.

I walked and walked, huge numbers of kilometres each day. We were heading into winter, and I'd wrap myself in my big coat and traverse our neighbourhood three, sometimes four times an evening. Hours of walking. A marathon of time.

Through it all, I thought about that filtered image of motherhood. I'd been to see a doctor about the thoughts I'd been having, and she'd wasted no time in telling me sternly, *I can't prescribe you anything for it; it's not good for the baby.* Instead, she gave me a referral to a psychologist and told me it would be worth it in the end. *Silly girl,* I could hear her thinking, her unsmiling lips pursed at me. I went home and booked an appointment for two weeks later (*fourteen days, fourteen days*) and hoped I wouldn't kill myself before then.

I hated that doctor for being so dismissive and for telling me things I knew weren't true. But I tried to believe what she had said. That it would be worth it in the end. That peace would come from being free of the thing and seeing the thing turn into a baby. My baby. I told myself I would love him instantly, and it would all be okay. I cried in the shower thinking about it, listening to songs that I hoped would bridge the gap between this broken me and the me that would soon be made whole. I listened to 'Ain't No Mountain High Enough', singing it to the thing in the hope it would hear my voice and understand on some level what I was trying to say: *You are on the other side of this nightmare, baby, but I'm coming for you.* I listened to

Tim Minchin's 'When I Grow Up', imagining the thing as a child with dreams and hopes and a personality of its own, but a need still for a mother who loved them and always would no matter what.

But the love is what I worried about most of all. In fact, it was the thing that set the panic off in the first place. I had been away for the Easter long weekend with my girlfriends, one of whom had a four-month-old baby I adored. Lying in bed when I got home, I had a sudden thought: *What if I don't love my baby as much as I love Freddy?*

I tried to push the thought away, but the poison had already found its way through the cracks. If I didn't love my baby—'the thing', as it had become in my mind—I would still be stuck with it. It would sense my lack of love early on, and it would grow up knowing I had withheld it from them. I couldn't help but damage the child, I thought, because I would force on it the horrendous perfectionism that I had placed on myself throughout my life. I would blame it for how it reflected on me, the way I had felt similarly implicated throughout my life by a father troubled by his own parents' rigidly high standards.

I had wanted a baby for superficial reasons, thinking I had an abundance of love to give and wanting to know what it felt like to care more for someone else than I did for myself. But I began to fear that I was an unfeeling person, someone capable of great cruelty and whose care was given conditionally. A person who would make a small, innocent creature work hard for their love and punish them in various ways when they came up short.

Unable to resolve the problem of it all, I walked and I cried and I hoped. And all the while, the thing inside me grew.

♥

One of the most pressing things she teaches him to do after the first lockdown begins is to wash his hands properly. She shows him how to wash the palms and then each finger, rubbing them together into a big, soapy lather. She's paranoid about surfaces, flinching whenever he touches anything outside the confines of their small apartment. She knows the virus isn't supposed to affect small children . . . but still.

She makes up a song for him, singing it to the tune of the Spice Girls' 'Stop Right Now', and he performs it for her theatrically.

Stop right now!
Don't ya go outside!
The time has come for us to stay inside and hide!
We're all doing what we can
That's why we've all got to wash our hands!

They make up games together, running up and down the hallway, playing hide-and-seek and using the brooms from the closet to mock fight with each other.

Sometimes the fighting is for real. They live on top of each other with nowhere to go and nothing to do, and she can't be upbeat all the time. She tries to hide in her room, but he finds her.

'Come sit with me,' he pleads.

She wants to be kind because she knows this is just as confusing for him as it is for her, but she's annoyed too. There are days she doesn't *want* to be a mother in a pandemic, days when she wishes her problem was not enough human touch instead of too much of it. She can see herself being short-tempered, feel herself pushing him away, and she hates herself in those moments.

Hey! her internal voice commands. *Calm down! It's okay! Take a deep breath. This is not as bad as you're making it out to be.*

Shut up, you! she screams back at the voice.

She berates herself for it on the phone to Alice, who has done her own share of yelling at children during the unexpected shutdown of the entire world. They pour their guilt down the phoneline, laying bare all their worst crimes and unfeeling thoughts for each other to witness. And then they agree to each other to forgive themselves, the way mothers have always needed to in order to survive the intensity of the role.

❣

My dream of the foundling all those years ago had made me believe that a mother was born at the same time her child arrived into the world. That the fact of motherhood itself was what turned her from an ordinary human into an unrelenting soldier, Sarah Connor transformed from meek and mild girl to a ripped machine with an arsenal of weapons tasked with protecting her child at all costs.

But I was wrong in thinking that this was the sum total of what being a mother felt like; that it began in the same place it ended, an infinite circle looping back and forth between being someone's shield and being their sword.

I was a mother before my son was born, when he was the thing still growing inside me, when I didn't feel that way about him at all. I was a mother in the hours before his birth, when I turned up to the hospital with a bag of clothes and a book. We sat together in the waiting room, me and the book, before they hooked me up to tubes to send drugs coursing through my body that made my pelvis feel like it was being crushed in a vice. I was no less a mother when I demanded the epidural so I could spend the next few hours blissfully pain-free before the time came to push and he was suddenly tearing out of my body, leaving it wounded and weeping. I was a mother when they whisked him to the resuscitation table to clear his airways of the meconium he was covered in. I remember gazing down at him when they finally placed him on my chest, the tubes tangling around us both like brambles, my throat still raw from the howls of anguish I'd unleashed during his passage into this world, the centre of me strangely empty now that he was no longer pushing all of my organs into my extremities.

Don't touch me, I thought, my head flopping to the side of the pillow, a mother then too.

I was a mother when we brought him home (I forgot the book, sadly) in all his gnarled need, erupting at me whenever I put him down, screeching for milk, for comfort, for warmth.

I gave him these things mostly because I didn't want him to suffer, but also because I wanted him to stop screaming at me. I didn't know how to do anything, and learning on the job was, to be frank, very stressful.

I was a mother when I walked gingerly through the house, leaking into concealed incontinence pads and sometimes through them and into my underwear, my body weeping tears for the loss of control over itself and feeling like not even a spin dry on a *very* hot heat would ever shrink my vagina back to its original size. I was a mother when I told the maternal health care nurse that I was concerned about the state of my pelvic floor, and she handed me a government-issued leaflet with the title '1 in 3 Mothers Wet Themselves After Birth', and I was a mother when I bought a bizarre-looking vibrator that claimed it would tighten your vaginal walls through electrical stimulation but which looked like it fell off the back of a truck. I put it in a cupboard—unused—and threw it away when the next hard rubbish collection came around.

I was a mother when I screamed at my partner one night that 'I need a grown-up!' and I was a mother when he replied, 'Clementine, *you're* the grown-up now.'

I hadn't pictured any of this in the lead-up to his arrival, infused as my fantasies were by those pastel dreams of maternity I had fixated on in the beginning. I remembered the image of us lying peacefully together on the quilted bedspread I'd bought, him sweetly cooing while I lazily read books and occasionally napped. In my visions, he would entertain me when I was in the mood and go to sleep without protest when I wasn't.

Who was this wrinkled, howling creature and where was the baby I had been promised?

There was so much I hadn't been told about what this new reality would look like, and of course I had never thought to ask anyone who'd been through it themselves.

Perhaps the biggest surprise to me was that I wasn't allowed to sleep, not even following the terrible, horrible, no good, very bad birth. By the time he eventually made his appearance, I had been more or less awake for thirty-six hours, and—spoiler—babies don't care if you're tired. I had heard the rumours they rarely slept, or slept sporadically and at odd hours of the day. But I didn't fully appreciate, *couldn't* fully appreciate, that when people say that babies mean you never sleep again they mean you actually literally *never sleep again*, or at least don't sleep for such a long time that it may as well be eternity. In preparation for the baby's arrival, I had bought a monstrously expensive and elaborate baby hammock that my friend's child had just *loved*. He'll sleep in that, I thought, which will leave me time to potter around and get some work done. Maybe I'll learn a language, become proficient in French or Spanish. Oh yes, I'd say, I learned to *hablas* while I was wafting beatifically around our neat apartment that never smelled like baby poo and in which I never looked at my partner and thought, *You fucking BASTARD, I hate you.*

Reality was a rude shock. The baby hated the fancy hammock, and the sidecar bassinet I'd bought to replace it, and the DockATot after that, and whatever else the internet assured me would help him—and therefore me—to sleep. He preferred to remain attached to me at all times. I succumbed to a baby carrier and the hammock sat there, gathering dust and holding piles of laundry until I finally sold it a few months later.

I didn't know about cluster feeding, which happens in the first few weeks of a baby's life, when they eat like zombies for hours at a time in an attempt to ensure their own survival by stimulating steady milk supply. My nipples were often left cracked and bleeding, so much so that one night I looked down at him to see blood smeared across his lips as he furiously ate from me.

I hated so many of these new experiences, and in those moments I thought that meant that I hated him.

I was a mother through all of this. And was it love? Not the kind we are taught to expect. There was no depth to it, no light or shade. Those days were about survival. I had survived a crushing pregnancy and a traumatic birth. Now I needed to somehow find a way to help the creature responsible for those things to survive in the world. To survive *me*, as I figured out how to forgive him for the ways I had been irrevocably changed and to understand that they were never his fault.

❣

On the rarest of occasions, in the small space they share, she finds herself utterly bewildered by the continued presence of this small creature. Not in the context of gratitude. *How did I get so fortunate? What did I do to deserve such a blessing of a child?* Nothing like that, although of course she feels all those things too, profoundly and almost constantly.

This is a different feeling, and she assumes most mothers have had it on at least one occasion, if they're paying attention. It's the unsettling sense of having slipped out of the normal run of things; of glancing up in the middle of an ordinary moment on an otherwise unremarkable day and feeling suddenly as if you might have amnesia. You look at this child you have borne, the one whose limbs and freckles and hair you assembled inside you, whose personality grew alongside those things and whose very landscape you seem to have memorised a million times over: the peach fuzz that covers their shoulders; the birthmark that glows beneath chestnut hair on the nape of their neck; the way their legs bow ever so slightly. You look at the collection of these things presented by a child who stands before you asking for something in a voice it feels like you've known your entire life, and still, for the briefest of moments, the entire world falls away and you find yourself thinking, *Who are you and what are you doing in my house?*

She hadn't felt this sensation for a long time—not since the days in which the boy was still distinctly *baby*—but it hits her again in the second week of Melbourne's third lockdown, the one known as stage 4, where they were confined to a five-kilometre radius of their home. She is standing in the kitchen, grabbing keys and a bag and a jacket and everything else you need to leave the house with a small child in the middle of winter. He barrels up the hallway behind her yelling, 'Mum, Mum! Guess what?'

Before she can even try to guess, there he is telling her: 'I put my mask on myself!'

She looks at him, and something about his face being concealed combined with the hangover that's beginning to prick at the corners of her vision (the hangover caused by her new and not entirely unwelcome bottle-of-wine-a-night habit) instantly destabilises her.

Who are you? she thinks. And she knows who he is, of course she does, but in that moment she also understands clearly how some people can believe the FBI has bugged their phone or is trying to mind-control them through the radiation that comes out of their microwave. She can *feel* the intoxicating shimmer of paranoid delusion beckoning to her, telling her the things she can see and touch and smell and taste aren't real, that everything she knows and loves in this world is a lie. She sees the possibility of that stretching out before her, rising like a tidal wave and threatening to drag her to the bottom of the ocean.

She grabs a chair to steady herself, sucks in a deep breath of air and forces herself to act as if everything is normal.

Is it? Isn't it?

The boy skips happily down the hall and calls to her. They are going to the shops. They are allowed one hour.

'Hold my hand,' she says to him as they step onto the street.

❦

When my son was a toddler, his dad and I took him to our local pub for dinner. It was a balmy summer evening, and the burnt orange streaks that seem so unique to Melbourne sunsets were beginning to stretch across the sky. We ate in the beer garden and shared a bottle of wine and watched our boy as he played near one of the garden beds, carefully assembling and then disassembling little piles of tanbark. In a few months' time, I was going to tell my partner that I wanted to break up with him. But for now, on this particular night and with our beautiful baby gently exploring the world we had made for him, life seemed pretty good.

We set off for home down the narrow street that runs off Sydney Road, leaving behind the rattle of the trams. F___ had just started refusing to use his pram, preferring instead to walk alongside us. It made me nervous at first, but I was beginning to appreciate the convenience of not having to wrestle with the bulky stroller whenever we wanted to go anywhere. Besides, I liked having an independent child. And this was independence, wasn't it?

That street has always been irritatingly narrow. Most of the houses for the first few hundred metres are row cottages, which means everyone parks their cars out front, leaving the two-way traffic to battle it out for the remaining space. Because it exists as a thoroughfare between two major roads, it's frequently clogged with people who drive unnecessarily fast just to beat the queue.

We hadn't made it that far past the pub when F___ suddenly pulled his hand from my grasp and squealed, 'Mummy! Chase!'

Before I could stop him, he stepped off the kerb and stood between the bumpers of two parked cars. He turned to me, beaming.

'Chase!' he commanded again.

I froze, abject terror flooding my body. The world collapsed around me, until it was just the two of us floating in dark space. He was just far enough away from me that it would take more than a step or two to reach him, but I worried that if I broke into a run he would think we were playing. Instead, I did what all terrified parents do when confronted with their child's recklessness—I screamed at him.

'Don't move!' I roared. 'Come back here RIGHT NOW.'

I can still feel myself standing there, every muscle in my body tensed as I extended a shaking hand towards him. He had been startled by the way I'd yelled, the smile dropping from his face. I watched, horrified, as he fixed me with a defiant stare and then deliberately stepped out into the street.

This is the split second that can change everything. We get lucky, or we don't.

The moment he stepped into the thoroughfare, I bolted towards him and swept him up in my arms, clutching him to me like his life depended on it.

Which, of course, it did.

'You never, ever, ever, EVER go onto the road without holding Mummy's or Daddy's hand!' I said, with as much force as I could muster.

He buried his face in my neck and started to whimper. I clung to him, stroking his back and making soft *shhhhh*ing noises in his ear.

'Darling, you *frightened* me,' I whispered to him.

We were very lucky that night: that night on the narrow street with the cars you don't always see and the toddler who was testing his boundaries. We walked home, me holding F___ tightly against my chest the whole way. After he'd gone to sleep, I poured another glass of wine and sat outside in the still night air. I saw it happen over and over again, but with a different, terrible outcome. My child stepping into the street and into the path of a car moving too quickly; a driver not watching for the flash of small limbs. I saw it happen in a million different ways, a car coming this way or a car coming that, the end result always the same. Metal, tyres, the hot smell of burning rubber. A howl that comes up from the centre of the earth, located deep inside my belly.

A split second is all it takes for the world to become completely undone and then you're falling through space for eternity.

The author Elizabeth Stone once wrote 'Making the decision to have a baby is momentous. It is to decide forever to have your heart go walking around outside your body.' My friend Heidi had her own, simpler version of this realisation when she brought her daughter home eight weeks before the arrival of my son.

'It felt reckless to let myself love her,' she told me.

When my son was born, I understood implicitly what she meant. Because what if something happens to them? But as my love for him has grown, I understand this feeling of recklessness is not just about his vulnerability but about my own too.

To let yourself love someone so completely and so unconditionally is the biggest leap of faith there is. And the love that a child offers you in return—pure, glowing and free of malice or expectations—feels similarly dangerous. What have we done to deserve it, this love that asks nothing of us but to be met with grace? It is the first love I've ever had that makes me feel truly accepted and seen, and it terrifies me because I know how fleeting it is.

The love of a child is like the life cycle of a match. It sparks brightly, the flame bursting into the air in a giant bulb, fierce and strong, the smell of sulphur hitting your olfactory nerves and singeing you before the light itself settles to a steady flicker and we can be assured that the flame has held.

But no match burns forever.

My job is to protect the light of this love for the length of time that it takes me to pass it on to something else. A candle, a pile of kindling, a block of wood—anything in which it can live on, with no more need for me to cup my hand around it to shield it from the things that might snuff it out.

I had thought this feeling would abate as he grew older and more capable, but instead it has, just like him, continued to grow and change. Protecting the heart was once a matter of practicality. I feared turning my head for one second too long and him rolling down the stairs, out the door and back into the mystery from where he came. I worried about his busy hands picking up something I'd left lying on the ground—a cashew nut, a button, one of the endless bloody bobby pins that are scattered across the living room floor in the fall-out of attempts to tame one's hair—and him swallowing it. Tiny things that could crack a hole in the earth just big enough for him to tumble into and into which my giant, clumsy hands couldn't reach. But then came the bigger, scarier things to worry about—the maladies of his own heart, my outside heart. The slice of mean words and cruel children, the worry that he might be left out or bullied. And then later, years from now, the fear of a sadness or anxiety that might descend on him the way it has on me throughout my life.

What if, what if, what if?

In some ways, I will spend the rest of my life as a mother on that narrow road watching as he lifts his foot to step out onto a road whose dangers I cannot see.

Don't move! I scream internally.

But my outside heart has learned to walk, as all outside hearts must, and there's nothing I can do to stop it now.

❣

She and the boy ride the bicycle every day, up and down the streets of the neighbourhood. They're looking for bears, the furry teddies people have placed in their front windows to give the children something to do each day.

'Mummy!' he cries out excitedly each morning. 'Let's go look for bears!'

'Okey-dokey!' she replies. 'How many shall we try to find today?'

They settle on a number, and she straps him into his seat on the bike. Sometimes they sing songs and sometimes they talk about what they'll do later that day, with the limited options available to them. Often they ride in companionable silence, speaking up only to point out the bears that are, after all, the purpose of the outing. He is always blown away to find them, screaming it out to her so that she won't miss seeing this wonderful, miraculous thing.

'BEAR!'

Occasionally, she reaches behind her to tickle his tummy. He giggles in her ear.

'Mummy!' he peals. And then, after a pause, 'Again!'

Instead of tickling him, she lets out a deep burp.

'You did a burp!' he shrieks, joy pouring from him.

'I did!' she replies. 'Naughty Mummy!'

She then lets out an even louder one, and he erupts once more.

'Mummy,' he says, 'do knock knock.'

'Knock knock,' she says.

'Yes, who's there?' he answers.

'Mummy,' she replies.

'Mummy who?' he asks, giggling in anticipation.

'Mummy who loves looking for bears with her buddy,' I say.

'Knock knock!' he says.

'Who's there?' she replies.

'F___!'

'F___ who?' she asks.

'F___ who loves going swimming and eating ice cream!'

275

'These are good things to love,' she tells him.

'Mummy?' he says.

'Yes, my darling?' she calls back, glancing at him over her shoulder. He's nestled into the cushioned headrest of his seat.

'I love you in the whole wide world.'

If they ride late enough in the day, she will sometimes peer over her shoulder to see that he's nodded off, head bobbing in time with the spinning wheels of the bike. She wonders what he's dreaming about, being struck with the realisation once again that she knows very little about the inner workings of the person who has become the most important thing to her in all the history of the universe.

When he was a baby, only a few days old, she sat looking into his eyes one day on a couch that would soon enough be stained by food and milk. It seemed to her as if those eyes held the secrets of the cosmos, huge and inscrutable as they were. She announced this to the man standing behind her, the baby's father, and he came to peer over her shoulder at the extra-ordinary discovery.

Phrbbbbbbbbbbbththththt!

The noise erupted out of the baby's bum, and she felt the rumble of the milk poo vibrate through her hands. She and the man laughed, an unrestrained joy that would become rarer and rarer the longer they lived together and only return when the storms of separation had subsided and they could at last be friends.

Pedalling down the quiet Brunswick streets, she thinks to herself how grateful she is for these moments. Her world was very busy before the world itself ended. Now, she has learned to adjust her expectations, waiting for nothing from each day but exactly the same thing she experienced yesterday, the day before, last week—twenty years ago, for all she knows.

Slowly, they reach a new normal. They learn each other's moods and how to navigate them, to anticipate the corners so that they know when to pull against them and when to lean in. Sounds chime throughout the day to remind them what time it is. The doorbell buzzes to let them know a package has been left in the entrance hall. Their neighbours go out for a walk with their toddler and new baby, the one who was born at the very start of lockdown and who, because of this, has never been held by anyone other than her two mothers. The construction workers across the street pick up tools in the morning and put them down at the day's end. Even that burnt orange sunlight streaming through the windows in the late afternoon brings with it its own curious sound. Everything is slower and more still, especially her.

She thinks of those early days as they sit together in the living room with Lego strewn across the carpet, *Winnie the Pooh* playing on the TV for what might be the millionth time by now. They were in a different house then, with a different carpet, but the tableau was essentially the same: a mother and her child riding out the passing of the hours together, as the world outside drifts further and further away.

❣

'Why do you always say that?' my son asks me, a tiny sliver of something in his voice. Disgust maybe, or fear.

'What?' I ask, holding his hand as we walk to our local cafe.

'You always say that you love me,' he replies. He seems agitated, his brow furrowed slightly.

'Well,' I explain, 'because sometimes we have a feeling so big in our heart that we have to share it.'

'But I already *know* that you love me,' he says. 'You can only say it once a day, okay, Mummy?'

My heart stretches and bends to accommodate his wish, and I smile to cover the pain of it. My son is only four years old, and he already understands that love is a thing that can swallow you whole. The big feeling I need to share is too heavy for him to carry, pulling down on his limbs like heavy clothes worn in deep water.

'Okay, darling,' I reply. 'I'll just think it to myself instead.'

Later that night, lying next to him in bed, I whisper it to him again without thinking. *I love you.* But he doesn't recoil or worry, nor does he admonish me.

'Am I allowed to say it in bed?' I ask. 'When it's dark and we're snuggled up?'

He's quiet for a moment, but then he takes the thumb and forefinger of his right hand and shapes it into a tick. This is his way of saying yes to things when *his* feelings are too big inside him to form words.

In the dark, my love becomes a grounding force. It is the bed he sleeps in, the blankets that keep him from floating off into the atmosphere. It's the warmth of my body next to his, the steady breaths that tell him he's safe. I am the figure who lies between him and the door, the one who can protect him from everything that exists on the other side of it. The monsters that lurk in the shadows, the bad dreams, the lessons that are often hard to learn and so sometimes the scariest thing of all. I have heard him rallying himself at times, in the park or learning a new trick on his scooter. *Come on, F___! I hear him say. Be brave!*

But at night, surrounded by the love that pours out of me, he can finally relax. It must be like returning to the womb, a sensation of floating peacefully in love. When I realise this, I finally understand why he has always needed me to lie next to him to go to sleep. The nights he lay crying by himself in the dark when my overwhelming hatred of motherhood made it impossible for me to give that to him (and the guilt! the pointless guilt that I feel now that I can see more, know more!), the relief as I returned to him and held him, his sobs subsiding as he melted into me.

It has been a journey arriving here. Those early weeks of motherhood were so relentless and hard, ferrying him from the mystery to the moment. When I did finally recognise myself to be in love with him—unconditionally, enormously, transformatively—it wasn't with a thunderclap or a bolt. The love was quiet and spacious, like emerging from a late afternoon nap in a still room on a warm summer day and opening your eyes to marvel at how far the sun has moved across the sky.

Motherhood has been an endless business of learning some variation of this lesson over and over again. That what we think we know is not what we know at all. That love is at once messy and loud and absent and overwhelming and quiet and primal and inconvenient and terrifying *and and and*. We come to it with all the answers and discover early on that we must allow ourselves to surrender every last one of them to the ether.

I have been completely undone by mothering. But the fragments return piece by piece, each of them changed, the cracks that mark their separation a ravine of memories and wishes and dreams, always more dreams.

To love my child is to live in a constant state of collapse and repair, the fibres of my being torn apart every second and woven back together. I hold him to me sometimes during this eternal process of cellular renewal and find myself wishing the jaws of my body could inhale him and return him to the source of his creation; to those quiet, safe waters where he can never be hurt, never experience loss or grief, never be shown how immensely painful life can be and never, ever compound my own experience of this by growing to hate me.

But one of the many lessons I'm learning as a mother is how to accept that my love cannot be an anchor that drags him beneath the waves. Rather, it must be the deep water itself, buoyant and clear, for him to float in, to swim through, to carry him in its currents to shore when it is time for him to leave it as he surely one day will, as he surely one day must.

I have learned so many lessons about love through the gift of having my son, but by far the hardest one is this: that this big love, the biggest I have had and ever will have, is fleeting. It is the only kind of love we seek in which the purpose is for it to one day leave us.

The mark of my love lies in how willing I am to let it go.

❣

When her son was born, she reached into the deepest, most primal part of herself to bring that baby out into the open. I remember her screaming, 'I can't do this!' Her midwife gripped her hand and said, 'You *are* doing this!' She pushed harder, dug deeper than she thought she was capable of doing, and then breathlessly, incredibly, there he was.

Afterwards, when the room had emptied of people and instruments and blood, so much blood, her partner asked her, awestruck, 'How did you know how to do that?'

'I didn't!' she cried. 'I didn't!'

❣

I meet her on a bridge at sunset, the bridge I stopped at years ago to take a photograph with the man who would become the boy's father. It was late summer, and we had caught the exact moment the sun drops towards the horizon to rent the sky and give us a momentary glimpse of what lies in the dazzling beyond. In the photograph, our faces are bathed in orange flame.

She arrives in the moment at last, and I hold her close.

'You're here,' I whisper to her. And then it's just me, standing there and gazing out across the rooftops.

Nothing lives in the beginning forever, not even loneliness. Not even despair. The stories go on. We are writing them, even when we don't know how they'll end.

She is the one who tells me this on the bridge that day, that girl who has come so far, who went to the mystery to bring back the child who was hers, who was ours, who would one day be the world's. I will remember this wisdom with a future me in a future moment, when I meet them on the other side of a story, one in a long line of stories. There will be more lockdowns. There will be more life. All of these versions of me are stretched out across time witnessing it for each other, holding space for the ones yet to arrive, waiting to share what it is we've learned, waiting to discover what it is we do not yet know.

There is love in this place, just like there is love everywhere we care to look for it. There is beauty and there is hope and there is a boy and there is a mother and there is the past and there is the future but most importantly there is the now, and everything that exists between them that has got them from one moment to the next. The now is where we find the golden glow where, for the briefest of moments, the sky rips open and we see what it is we are made of.

Tell me a story, he asked me.

And so I began.

EPILOGUE

Dear Little Clementine,

It's me, you. That is to say, it's you, me. You'll understand one day. For now, I have some things to tell you.

First, I love you. So much. You are exactly who you're meant to be at this precise moment in time. Never doubt that you deserve to live in the world, and to be nourished and changed by all the things it has to offer, both the good and the bad. You have as much right as anyone else to live as if you're the main character.

Second, it's all going to be okay. You are going to have a wonderful life. There will be times when you might not feel like that's true, but trust me on this. There are times when you might not feel like you'll make it to the end, but you will. Even in the darkest hours, the earth will keep circling the sun and you will keep moving with it.

You will love, fiercely and completely. You already know that, though, because love is a wild creature whose call you can hear deep inside you. What you doubt is that this call will ever be heard by another, and that you will be loved in return.

Take heart, dear girl. You will be loved, and you will be known. Love will fill your life in ways you can't imagine. And even though your heart will sometimes break because of the weight of this love, the cracks it leaves behind are, as they say, how the light gets in.

One of the most wonderful things I've learned about life is how constantly surprising it is. You imagine it now as a linear thing, and because of this you'll spend some of your years climbing towards what you think is a happy conclusion. You expect that you will reach it when you're still young, and that all that remains is to slide towards the end, but you should know that things will not turn out exactly as you expected—and you will wake up every day feeling grateful for this. The climb as you imagine it doesn't exist at all. Your journey will involve peaks and some troughs, but every stage will show you something new. Because of this, you'll learn that life is wild and unpredictable, and that you can be wild and unpredictable too if you let yourself believe it.

People will move in and out of your life, and this is just the way things are. You'll say goodbye to friends and lovers and even enemies who no longer serve you, and pave the way for new people who'll love you in different ways and teach you more things you need to learn. Some of these partings will make you weep. Others will be welcomed and celebrated. None of them will leave you worse off than you were before, because all of it will tell you something about yourself.

There will be hard times.

One day, you'll have to say goodbye too early to the most important person in your life, and the pain you feel will seem insurmountable. But even from this, you will learn. You'll learn that love remains even when people are gone. It lives inside us and around us, and nothing can change that, not even death. You'll come to understand that the theft of more time doesn't change the fact it was a gift to have any time at all. Grief is proof that we have loved, and it can be beautiful if we let it be.

When you're a mother yourself (yes, joy will come to you in that way too), an old friend who you haven't seen for a long time will re-enter your life. He'll share with you a photograph, taken when you were nineteen. You'll look at her and see all the things she couldn't. That she was brave. Beautiful. Determined. That she belonged to the world, even if she didn't believe the world wanted her.

She thinks that love means being chosen, and that because of this she'll always miss out. You'll want to tell her that her worth and value as a human being is not dictated by whether she has a romantic attachment to someone else. She exists even if there's no one else there to witness it. She matters, even if there's no one else there to say so.

You'll look at her in this age of vulnerability and think of all the incredible things that are headed her way. The fierce rush of emotions, the heartbreaks, the mistakes she'll make, the triumphs she'll have, the hard lessons and the simple joys. You'll see in her the woman she's going to become and understand, finally, that it was in her all along. You'll thank her for bringing you to this point, for weathering that storm so you could emerge on the other side, fortified and indestructible.

Dearest little Clementine. Love can be found in the strangest of places. The heart is a muscle that pumps blood through the body, your body, that breathes and feels and moves and deserves kindness and love, especially love, especially from you.

The heart is a home, your home, and you can fill it with all the things that make a home a haven. Warmth. Solace. Sunlight. Books. Laughter. Nourishment. Snacks in the cupboard. Photographs on the walls. A soft place to land. A strong foundation to withstand the elements. You can wake up in your heart, your home, every day. Stretch, unfurl, potter around, water the plants, play some music, dance, breathe, commit to doing something about the shoes in the hallway but know that it doesn't matter, not really, because this is your home and a little bit of mess is what makes a home lived in.

Your heart is a map, a record of where you've been and where you're going. Your heart is a compass, guiding you in the right direction. Your heart is a journal, a memoir, a collection of stories. Some of them will make you cry. Some of them will feel bruising. Some of them you'll never be able to read again.

But some of them will make you laugh. Some of them will remind you of how strong you've been, and help you marvel at the hero you've become. And some of them will teach you what you already knew, deep down in your heart, in the tin can of treasures you buried beneath a loose floorboard so long ago.

Love is a symphony. Your heart is a conductor. Love is a question. Your heart is the answer.

See you soon x

ACKNOWLEDGEMENTS

There's no such thing as a book written by a single person, and this book is proof of that. I couldn't possibly have brought it to life without the hard work, encouragement and practical support of so many people. I feel extraordinarily privileged to have such an incredible team in my corner.

First and foremost, and as ever, thanks must go to my incomparable publisher, Jane Palfreyman. You are truly a force. You have championed me since the very beginning, and I will never forget it. Whither thou goest, I will go, for as long as you'll have me. Here's to many more bottles of wine, rantings about the state of the world, and brilliant collaborations!

To the brilliant and patient Christa Munns, who always tolerates my missed deadlines with kindness and grace, gently prodding me when necessary and using her stern email voice when I *really* needed it. I feel so grateful for your guidance and clever eye, and I don't know what I would do without you.

To Ali Lavau, who has once again provided me with an exceptional edit. You have the remarkable skill of always knowing which parts need to be streamlined, and which of my darlings need to be killed. Thank you for making the decisions for me so that I don't have to, and for being so wonderfully intuitive about the text.

Jane, Christa and Ali—it is an enormous privilege to have had the same core team work on the words with me for all three of my books. I feel truly bereft at the thought of losing any of you, because how could I trust anyone else to know me as well as you three do? Therefore, I forbid you from abandoning me and breaking my heart in the cruellest way. I forbid it!

Jacinta di Mase, my agent, my advocate, my pocket rocket general. You know how I feel about you. My life changed the day you agreed to have coffee with me in a Brunswick cafe, and I love you more deeply than you'll ever know. Here's to many more books, garden glasses of bubbles, and leopard print furs!

To Louise Cornegé, my manager and, more importantly, my dear friend. Thank you for keeping all the balls in the air so that I don't have to. I love that we end every conversation on the phone by saying, 'I love you', which is just as it should be.

To my publicist, Isabelle O'Brien, who from the outset was on the same page about how I wanted to talk about this book and who I wanted it to reach. I'm looking forward to post-event drinks with you in hotel bars and learning all about *your* love stories.

To Fleur Hamilton and Sarah Barrett, the marketing geniuses! It is no mean feat to sell a contemplative work on love and interior landscapes from a woman notorious for being combative. Thank you for taking on the challenge with gusto and vigour!

Christa Moffitt, you should know that when I first saw the cover design for the book, I *gasped*. You have captured everything I think this book is trying to articulate—that life is full of colour and hope, and there is something in it for all of us. Thank you for giving my book a face.

Pam Dunne, you crossed the T's and dotted the I's perfectly with your proofreading. I can be guilty of missing the little things, and you helped bring them to my attention. Thank you for your diligence and keen eye.

Rare parts of this book were written in my own house, but for the most part—at their generous invitation—I wrote at other people's kitchen tables, and in their caravans, warm living rooms and even a gorgeous converted tram. My deepest thanks to: Cat and Lucas McGauran, your kitchen took me back to year ten socials and broken hearts; Ange Henley, I unlocked everything I was trying to say about motherhood and isolation in the belly of beautiful Jean Claude Van Tram (may he ride again!); Jeanie Faure, the unexpected offer of your caravan brought the final pages of this book together, and I felt my mother there beside me—a true gift, and one I'll never forget; to Matt and the crew at Lobbs Cafe, thank you for indulging me as I drank endless cups of coffee and tapped away at a corner table. The love and magic you all weave with these spaces has found its way into this book, and I hope that in drawing from its well, I also managed to leave some of my own behind for the next person.

To the incredible educators and carers at Shirley Robs. Thank you for the work you do educating children, caring for them and teaching our littlest humans what it means to love and be kind. I could not have devoted the time needed to write this book without you all taking care of my most important love, and I will be forever grateful. Also, to Poppy Lifton, who has stepped in at the last minute so many times to care for the small one.

To the #hagarmy! Thank you for being my online family. You all got me through a long and lonely lockdown! Thank you for being my community, my readers, my friends. May we always be strong and true, and hold the line together.

I am lucky to love and be loved by so many wonderful women. Amy Thunig—I have clocked more hours on the phone with you than I can count, and long may it continue. Emily Ohanessian—here's to many more years of important science work in the egg lab. Mellissa Fyfe—I couldn't have chosen a better woman to be my son's godmother, and you will always be my godsister. Hannah Douglas—you were the best thing to come out of a break-up, and everyone should have one of you. Charlotte Ford, my actual sister and the best woman I have ever met. Karen Pickering, who loves Taylor and Tom as much as I do and who knows everything there is to know about me. To Clare Bowditch, who I have been lucky to love as a musician and even luckier to love as a friend. Clare, your song about grief played in my head on repeat as I wrote 'Starships'. Thank you. Libby O'Donovan, I will never be your shunt but I will love you forever and always. Naomi Wilson, who keeps me in awe with her bravery every day. You are all my family, and you have all taught me what it means to love.

I love some men too, despite rumours to the contrary! To Abe, who keeps me in stitches and will never let me forget about the time I asked if my Wikipedia page counted as a form of identification. To Houston, who I hope continues to join me in martinis and mayhem, and always thinks of me as a ratbag. To Harry, who is not a man but can be as bewitched by them as I can. To Julian, who has known me since the beginning. You are all magic.

To my father, Steven. Thank you for loving strong women. Thank you for raising them.

To my mother, Luciana. I will never stop missing you, but I'm so glad to have been loved by you. Your grandson and I often look for you in the rainbows and the waves.

To Alice Robinson. May we spend many afternoons on the banks of rivers talking about boys, and never lose the enthusiasm we have for each other. I love you more than any silly boy ever will.

To Jesse, my co-pilot and co-parent. No matter how the story has changed, we made the best boy in the world. Thank you for showing him what gentle love looks like, and for honouring me as his mother in all that you do. Thank you for being my family, now and forever and ever.

Finally, to those who continue to hope in the face of darkness. Humanity can be cruel and terrible, and life can bring out the worst in us all.

But my goodness! *How we love!*